BIG DADDY'S TALES
From the Lighter Side of
RAISING A KID WITH AUTISM

Never before published hilarity, favorite posts from the blog,
marginally helpful tips, poorly drawn cartoons galore, and oodles
of original stories from some of Big Daddy's favorite bloggers.

F.   Lewis   Stark

Introduction by Lynn Hudoba

Foreword by Melissa Harrison, PSY.D

ISBN: 1456565826
ISBN-13: 9781456565824
Library of Congress Control Number: 2011901264

Introduction

Lynn Hudoba
www.autismarmymom.com

Like all special needs parents, I experienced every stage of grief several times over when my daughter was first diagnosed with autism. Sometimes all in the course of the same day. I experienced denial, anger, depression, pain, and eventually acceptance. Ah, yes. Acceptance, the Holy Grail of the stages of grief. Every time that I cried a river, gnashed my teeth, wrung my hands, shook my fist at the skies, and asked "Why me?" it was all part of the process that was to ultimately bring me to acceptance. But even that doesn't sound like much fun, does it? What about happiness? What about joy? What about laughing 'til you squirt your drawers?

That's where Big Daddy comes in.

I was first introduced to Big Daddy's writing back in the late summer of Ought-9. I, a grizzled veteran blogger of more than four months; he, a young upstart. As I am wont to do with all new bloggers, I resolved to crush him into oblivion. I accomplished this by reading every one of his posts from day one, subscribing to his feed, anxiously awaiting for notification of every new post, and commenting on nearly all of them. Oh yeah, and laughing my ass off the whole way through.

What a relief to find a special-needs parent who could so effectively write about this journey of raising an autistic child without pathos, preachiness, or controversy. Big Daddy and I share the perspective that there is much joy and humor to be mined from lives with our extra-special children. To read Big Daddy, is to love his amazing son, Griffin. Alternately hilarious, maddening, endearing, and relentlessly curious, Griffin is a force to be reckoned with. The first comment that I ever wrote to Big Daddy was "I already love Griffin, and I'm only a few posts in." I know that you will feel the same way. Enjoy.

Foreword

Melissa Harrison, Psy.D.
Licensed Psychologist
Behavioral Health Institute

I was honored when F. Lewis Stark asked me to write this foreword. *Big Daddy's Tales from the Lighter Side of Raising a Kid with Autism* offers a unique perspective on how family life can be when living with an autistic child because it looks at dealing with stressful moments from the lighter side of life. I think this book fills a void that is not offered by any other book on the market because, in addition to discussing many common experiences that families have when they have a child with autism, it also offers hope by showing how humor and acceptance are effective ways of coping with these challenges. I am not only speaking from the professional's perspective but also as a parent of a child on the autistic spectrum. As a parent, I have found the stories in this book to be extremely helpful and validating of my own experiences.

My work with special needs kids began when I worked for the School District of Broward County in Fort Lauderdale, Florida, the sixth largest school district in the nation. I was hired as a school psychologist to provide psychological and psycho-educational testing to children. My job also included being part of the school-based team at the schools where I worked, which determines whether the children meet eligibility requirements for an individualized educational plan or IEP. Part of my work in the school district was evaluating children who were found to have autistic-spectrum disorders. One of the schools had a preschool with special needs children, many of whom had autism. I also have been working in private practice at Behavioral Health Institute in Coral Springs, Florida, since 1999. My private practice work with children has included helping children on the autistic spectrum, as well as their families, by providing evaluations and individual and family psychotherapy. Through therapy, I have given support, education, and assistance by helping children and their families to expand their skills, as well as guide families in working with the school system.

I highly recommend this book to families of children with autism-related disorders to help them cope, provide optimism, and recognize some of their own experiences within the book. I also recommend this book to professionals who assist these children and their families, not only so they can add the book to their biblio-therapy collection and recommend it to families, but also to better understand the daily challenges that these families face.

Dr. Melissa

Preface

In the beginning, Big Daddy created a blog. He called it big-daddyautism.com. And it was good. Then he wrote this book. About the blog. And other stuff. And it, too, was good. Then Big Daddy napped. And it, too, was good. Then Big Daddy wrote this preface. And, at that point, it all kind of started to fall apart for him. So then Big Daddy wrote a prologue.

Prologue

As I, Big Daddy, type this, my oldest son, Griffin, is peeking over my shoulder with an ear-to-ear grin plastered on his freckled face. Griffin, who just turned thirteen, is almost always smiling. He must have inherited this cheerful birth defect from his mother because I have spent most of my life in a perpetual grimace. Scowling seems to be my default setting. It's my signature look.

Even when I am happy, I frown. Smiling hurts my cheeks and looks painfully unnatural on me. Griffin's mom, on the other hand, smiles enough for the both of us. In fact, she still proudly lives up to her childhood nickname of Sunny. I, thankfully, have outgrown my childhood nickname of Blotchy, which was lovingly given to me as a fifth grader because of the half-dollar sized birthmark in the shape of the U.S.S.R. I sported like a fresh hickey on my neck. Sunny floats in and the room becomes brighter. Blotchy stomps around closing blinds, blowing out candles, and turning off lights.

Griffin is in an especially good mood as he contorts his neck to get a better look at my monitor. He has just re-turned from riding the elevator with his mom and sister at Macy's. Elevator rides always seem to brighten his day. Still craning and straining for a clearer view, he excitedly asks me if the words I am writing are all about him. They are—sort of.

Like the blog, this book is, above all else, about acceptance. I've thrown in a bit of gratitude, optimism, and perseverance in the face of adversity as well. There is also a bunch of amusing Griffin stories in here, and I've included some musings about perspective and spirituality as well. Most of all, this is a book about accepting what life has given us…and laughing at it.

Griffin is autistic. He does not suffer from a mild case of this condition, and he is not particularly high functioning like someone living with Asperger syndrome. Griffin is not just inattentive, distracted, or hyperactive. I could sugarcoat it by saying he is merely developmentally challenged, differently abled, or gifted. But the truth is, no matter what label we use, Griffin is significantly hindered and disabled by this perplexing disorder. Every minute of every day autism is a huge part of our lives.

Early on I saw Griffin's condition as a curse. I was certain that raising a kid with a disability like his would mean day after day of wretched misery. All gray skies and gloom. Decades of emotional pain and agony, here I come.

When we first heard his diagnosis, it felt like getting smashed with a frying pan to the face. It was as though we were handed a death sentence for a crime we did not commit. And this was all before we even began to contemplate the financial burden we now faced. Big Daddy has never been a big fan of financial burdens.

If I rarely grinned before, this surely would not help me get a nickname like Sunny or Smiley or even Moderately Content Dude. Funny thing is, I find myself beaming a good deal more than ever nowadays. Don't get it twisted—I'm still not skipping around like Richard Simmons on meth, but at least no one's calling me Dr. Death.

The Land of Clogs, Windmills, Tulips, and Cheese

Shortly after Griffin was first diagnosed, which was around his second birthday, someone gave us a tattered copy of a short story by Emily Perl Kingsley in which she compares raising a disabled child with a trip to Italy. It seems that every one in the "disability world" has a strong opinion about Ms. Kingsley's story. Some hate it, and some love it. Either way, here is Big Daddy's shortened version of the tale.

In the parable, the pregnancy is analogous to the trip planning stage while the birth and rearing of the child is the actual visit to Italy. The story goes something like this:

When you first become pregnant, it is like beginning to plan an amazing trip to Italy. While you are plotting out the journey, you get excited about all the wonderful things Italy has to offer. You research the restaurants where you will sample local foods, the museums you will visit, the ruins you will explore, and the high fashion stores in which you get to shop. You may even begin learning to speak some Italian. It's all very thrilling and even a little exhilarating. As the big day nears, you pack your bags, head to the airport, and get on the plane.

When the plane finally lands, the pilot announces over the intercom, *"Welcome to Holland."*

Stunned, frightened, and even a little embarrassed, you exclaim, *"Holland?!? There must be some mistake."*

Maybe you misheard the garbled voice of the captain. You are not supposed to be in Holland. You bought your tickets and packed specifically for Italy. You always dreamed of going to Italy and had never given Holland a thought. But, without your approval, there was a change in your flight plan, and you've landed in Holland.

After the initial shock and disappointment wears off, you start to realize that the place you have been taken is not what you had planned for, but it's not disgusting and horrible. It's just different. Not where you expected to go. So, now, you must get yourself new guidebooks and learn a whole new language. You will meet an entirely new group of people who also, to their surprise, landed in Holland. Some of these people planned their whole lives on going to Italy as well. Once you have been there for a while, get your bearings, and start to explore, it begins to dawn on you that Holland is pretty nice. It has charming windmills and vibrant tulips. Holland has also been home to some of the greatest artists of all time, like Escher, Van Gogh, and Rembrandt.

Even so, most people you know are busy traveling to and from Italy. They tell you, and everyone in earshot, how wonderful Italy is and how it exceeds their expectations. For the rest of your life, you must stay in Holland. You were supposed to go to Italy, too. That was not to be. If you spend your life mourning the fact that you did not get to go to Italy, you miss out on how beautiful Holland can be.

Ms. Kingsley's analogy has had a profound and long-lasting effect on my wife, Sonya, and me. On particularly difficult days with Griffin, when it feels as though we are forever tilting at windmills, Sunny and I sometimes turn to each other and say in unison, *"Holland sucks! I want to go to Italy!"*

Other times, there is nothing quite as beautiful as a day in Holland.

In a twist of fate, almost three years after the birth of our son, God gave us Hayden (Lil Sis for all you blog fans), a gorgeous and typical baby girl. Although our flight was originally diverted, we did get to go to Italy after all. So, in the end we got the best of both worlds. For that, we are eternally grateful and would not change any part of our trip.

Like the blog, this book is not a how-to manual. Nor is it meant as a *Raising an Autistic Kid for Dummies* book. It will not provide resources, but, we hope, if you look real close, you will pick up some practical advice along the way. However, I certainly will not proffer any legal, therapeutic, or medical advice upon which anybody should rely.

The purpose of this book is to show that raising a child with a disability is not all about sorrow, lost hopes, doctors, fighting insurance companies, avoiding quacks, miracle drugs, therapists, and the like. This book pays homage to the beauty and splendor of "Holland." A tribute to that incredible little kid we call Griffin who has brought us so much happiness and laughter. As anyone who has ever met Griffin can readily attest, the joy that he brings to this world far outweighs any of the sadness caused by his condition. Without exception, any person who has spent time with him has fallen in love with Griffin. So, in a way, this is a love story—Griffin's love story.

Taunting and Teasing the Handicapped Kid

In our family we use humor as a coping mechanism and also as a way to bring Griffin into our world. He understands and uses sarcasm, which, we have been told, is unusual for kids with his diagnosis. We try not to coddle or baby him. Quite simply, he is a member of the family, and he gets the same razzing we give each other. He rarely teases back as good as he gets. However, when he does zing someone, it is beyond awesome. Not only does making fun of him not hurt him, we think it makes him stronger.

For example, many times Griffin's compulsions are exhausting and draining for him and everyone around him. Occasionally, poking fun at him about his more obsessive behaviors dissuades Griffin from continuing them. Rather than caving in and playing along with his disruptive conduct, we mock him. By not giving him the response and feedback he desires, sometimes the unacceptable behavior ceases… at least temporarily. Griffin doesn't necessarily always find the humor in the situation, but we find it to be a gentle way to nudge him into more appropriate and tolerable behavior.

Best of all, we really enjoy it. We have discovered that, by finding and recognizing the humor in our lives, we are better able to survive it. Laughter allows us to move through tragic circumstances and is integral to our peace of mind. We choose to be optimistic because, well, it just feels better than wallowing in sorrow, grief, and self-pity.

The Downside

My intention is to keep the tone of my blog and this book upbeat, inspirational, and optimistic. However, it would be misleading if we did not admit that our life with Griffin has been difficult and challenging, to say the least. In the next paragraph or two you'll get a glimpse of the bad stuff so we can spend the rest of the time accentuating the good stuff. The fact that the downside can be summed up in under a hundred words, while the upside has provided hundreds of amusing blogs posts, should show you what we think about Griffin.

Griffin was diagnosed as autistic when he was about twenty-one to twenty-two months old. At the time he was neither walking nor talking and had exhibited many of the classic symptoms of autism, as well as a few that are not so typical. Griffin missed (and continues to miss) virtually every developmental milestone. Very early on, several specialists diagnosed him as having severe gross- and fine-motor impairment, as well as having significant speech and language deficiencies. He is hypo- and hypersensitive to touch and sounds. Sometimes, he cannot stand to be touched, while at other times he craves as much tactile input as possible.

Developmentally and socially Griffin, at thirteen, is much like a three-year-old. He has numerous repetitive behaviors, stims, and tics. These include arm flapping, facial twitching, severe nail biting, inappropriate giggling, hitting (himself), skin rubbing (until raw), pinching (himself and others), repeating (words or phrases over and over), rocking, head banging, and making strange noises. Griffin is clinically obsessive about certain things, and, at times, cannot be consoled if his schedule changes or seemingly trivial things do not go precisely as he wants.

Griffin's disability is not subtle, and it is constantly apparent. It interferes with his schoolwork, social relationships, and ability to perform basic life skills. He needs significant assistance with most things thirteen-year-old kids take for granted. As he ages, and his progress slows, it is becoming clearer that he (barring a miracle) most likely will never live independently and will continue to need intensive therapy.

Pop Some Popcorn,
Kick Back, and Enjoy the Show

In spite of the fact that it is not always easy, life with Griffin is, for lack of a better phrase, humorously bizarre. The odder it gets, the more interesting it is. We believe the only way to approach it is to kick back and enjoy the show. Similarly, we have decided the best way to share Griffin with the world is to recount some of his funniest and offbeat moments—anecdotes of our adventures in raising one of the quirkiest kids any of us has ever known.

The following are what we believe to be the best of the best. Our favorite posts, cartoons, and a ton of never before published material. As always, a few of the passages will lose something in translation from Griffin's unique speech patterns to the written word. A number of the stories can only be appreciated by those who know him well. However, we hope most of the anecdotes will be funny, inspirational, and maybe even helpful for other parents who are also blessed to be raising a child with special needs.

Some of the names, dates, and locations have been changed or slightly altered to protect the innocent, the nasty, and the embarrassed. Mainly they have been changed to protect me. I have taken a bit of artistic license in rearranging some of the events to provide more continuity, and I have recreated a portion of the dialogue from my sometimes-fuzzy memory.

Those familiar with Big Daddy's work will not be surprised to learn that his is not an exercise in journalism, and I do not pretend to be an investigative reporter. I may have added some hyperbole here and there. However, when it comes right down to it, I think the following is a fairly accurate glimpse at our life with Griffin.

Elevator Safari

And Then There Was Screaming

Game On

He never really cried as a baby. Griffin screamed, screeched, and shrieked quite a bit, but he never cried. Crying doesn't, as far as I know, make your parents' ears bleed. Griffin spent virtually every waking moment of the first year of his life in a state of full on hysteria. We used to pray for plain old colic or crankiness. Fussy babies made us envious beyond imagination. (Mia Farrow had it easier in *Rosemary's Baby*.)

When he was born, the nurses at the hospital would apologetically wheel our beautiful bundle of joy into our room in that ubiquitous transparent-acrylic-bubble-infant pod telling Mrs. Big Daddy that they knew she needed some rest, but Griffin was screaming so loudly that it was waking up all the other babies in the nursery. He needed to spend some time in our room so that the other newborns could get a little sleep. It was then that the sport of bubble pod tennis was conceived. This activity quickly became a deadly serious competition between us and the nursing staff in the maternity ward.

The match would commence with a not-too-cheerful overnight nurse wheeling the pod into Mrs. Big Daddy's room. After about two minutes of severe auditory damage, I would return their Agassi-like serve by rolling the pod back to the nursery. After Mrs. Big Daddy and I finally fell asleep, the nurse staff would deliver a crushing forehand smash down the line by sneaking the pod back in our room under the cover of darkness. Temporarily defeated, we would soon awaken to Griffin's screams and a new set would begin. I got a lot of exercise those few nights in the hospital. In the end, thanks mainly to strength in numbers and staying fresh because of shift changes, the nurses got the best of us.

The first night we brought him home, I kept instinctively looking for the pod so I could push Griffin back to the nursery in the desperate hope that some of the other residents in our apartment complex could get a little rest that evening. My sleep-deprived father-in-law must have wondered why I kept shouting, *"Game on nurses! Game on!"*

Adventures in Dining

Mrs. Big Daddy and I used to dine out quite frequently. This, of course, was before Griffin was born. In fact, we virtually stopped visiting restaurants altogether for the first two to five years of his life. This saddened us deeply since we were very good at eating out.

Celebrity Chef Roco DiSpirito has said that the restaurant business is all about chaos and drama. However, *chaos* and *drama* don't come close to describing what Griffin would bring to a bistro. To say, as a baby, Griffin was difficult in eateries would be like saying Florida gets a little warm and moist in August. Words do not give the experience justice.

In fact there are more than a few restaurants in which Griffin was banned for projectile vomiting, clearing tables without the assistance of a busboy, screaming without taking a breath for hours at a time, and discharging a firearm in the direction of the kitchen. Okay, I made that last one up, but we sometimes left restaurants looking like the entire road crew for Guns N Roses stopped by after a concert and were told the bar had run out of Jack Daniels.

We want to take this opportunity to extend a sincere apology to the Moon Light Diner in Fort Lauderdale for the events that took place during the lunch hour rush sometime in the summer of 1998. Please take Griffin's picture off your banned-for-life wall. Mrs. Big Daddy swears that the one french fry she got to scarf down before her eviction was delicious. We hear the remodeling and restoration went smoothly, and the place looks even better than before.

Battening Down the Hatches

It didn't take long for his pediatrician's staff to realize that Griffin was special and that it would be in everyone's best interest to move him through the well visits as quickly as possible. Sailors on a submarine know there are certain procedures that must be followed before the ship can submerge. Much like the seamen battening down hatches and manning their stations, the nurses in the doctor's office knew they needed to prepare for the arrival of Hurricane Griffin.

Despite our best efforts, things occasionally went awry. Vaccinations and blood tests were always tricky, so, since I used to be marginally stronger than Mrs. Big Daddy, I was elected to be the attending parent for the more physically demanding appointments. No child likes to have his finger stuck for a diabetes screening, but Griffin was able to turn this fairly routine procedure into a blood bath. Literally.

Griffin squirmed, wriggled, and squealed so much that, even though there was only one pinprick, my shirt wound up covered in blood. The nurses must have thought we had hit an artery. I left the office looking like an extra from the opening scene of *Saving Private Ryan*. I almost wish I had a fender bender on the way home just so I could have seen the reaction on the face of the other driver as I stumbled out of the car covered in blood.

Roller Coasters

A couple of years back, the Big Daddy clan decided to take a road trip to Orlando, home of Mickey and the $49.00 bottled water. Once we arrived, all Griffin wanted to do was ride roller coasters (and talk about elevators and Wilford Brimley).

Unfortunately, aversion to roller coasters is practically a family tradition for me. My dad claimed he could not ride them because of an unfortunate childhood penny incident. His story was that he still had a coin lodged in his nose from when he stuck it up there as a young boy growing up in Brooklyn. Therefore, he would purportedly bleed profusely from the altitudes and speeds sustained in the ride. Oddly enough, airplanes, elevators, and skyscrapers didn't seem to cause any hemorrhaging. Even weirder was that the doctors left the penny in his nose all these years. It wasn't like tweezers had yet to be invented when my dad was a kid.

It wasn't until I was well into middle age that I figured out that it was fear, not money in his snout, that kept my dad from riding Space Mountain. Because Griffin doesn't share his paternal ancestors' apprehension of amusement park attractions, I am often forced to break with tradition and ride with my son. By exposing myself to my fear of roller coasters, I have been able to overcome it. Somewhat. Unfortunately, I have not been able to overcome the dizziness, vertigo, and nausea. I literally turn green, which, when you are, say, visiting the Shrek area at Universal Studios in Orlando, isn't a good thing—especially if you are bald and weigh in at around 300 pounds.

While the kids wait in line to get a chance to meet Shrek, a mechanical version of his sidekick Donkey (voiced by a live comedian hidden from view doing a passable Eddie Murphy imitation), makes wisecracks. The jokes were mostly benign and inoffensive until I showed up all green faced, bald, and sweaty. At that point, Donkey let loose a tirade. His best line, according to the crowd reaction, went something like this: "Hey, Shrek. Ever wonder what you'd look like with a beard and an Iron Man T-shirt? Just look at that guy over there." Ba-dum-bum! Zinged by an animatronic ass.

Unlike Big Daddy, roller coasters do not make Griffin turn green. To the contrary, Griffin absolutely loves them, which is kind of ironic since a roller coaster is an apt metaphor for our life with him. Some people's lives are like a merry-go-round—boring, slow, and repetitive. Others are like a roller coaster—ups and downs. Exhilarating, terrifying, etc. Life with Griffin is like a monster roller coaster. Unlike the carousel folks, living with Griffin is never boring. Some people quietly slip through life unnoticed. Not Griffin. He is like that tremendous roller coaster you can see even before you park the SUV at the amusement park. I wouldn't have it any other way.

Chew on This

Griffin was never adept at getting nourishment from the bottle, but we really hit a roadblock when he started to move into solid food. He always had a huge appetite, but he didn't know how to chew. That's right, we had to teach

Griffin to chew. He could swallow just fine, but the act of mastication was foreign to him. For most of us, the process is simple and, for the most part, involuntary. We open and close our jaw, use our teeth to grind the food and our tongues and cheeks to move it around—not Griffin. Since, as author Fran Lebowitz has astutely noted, food is an important part of a balance diet and most food needs to be chewed, this was not a minor developmental issue.

When you need to teach your son how to chew, it sort of puts the other problems in life into perspective. It's hard to get riled up about a traffic jam when your baby cannot perform one of the most basic functions of being a human. Even your own health or money woes pale in comparison when you consider what the future has in store for a child who was born without the tools (or at least the user manual) necessary to get sustenance. Needless to say we don't do much fretting over grades and FCAT scores.

Mrs. Big Daddy spent countless hours physically moving Griffin's jaw up and down and side to side to simulate chewing until, one day, he finally got it—sort of. We cannot put our finger on it, but there is something still a little odd about the way he does it. Bugs Bunny chomping on his carrot and the Cookie Monster inhaling a bag of Chips Ahoy come to mind. Regardless, once he got a system that worked for him, Griffin became a chewing machine.

Get Out of Jail Free

Griffin's propensity for epic eruptions, and his inability to roll with the punches, has proven to be a blessing at times. Getting to graciously leave parties and similar functions early is always a nice perk. Mrs. Big Daddy and I love our friends and family, but we subscribe to the theory that social gatherings in small doses are almost always better than long affairs. For me, parties and get-togethers are like tuna sandwiches left outside in the midday sun. Even if they start out delicious, it doesn't take too long before they become rotten and rancid.

Most "normal" people can't leave a kid's birthday party before the cake is served (no matter how much they want to) without looking like a heel. But since Griffin's tantrums are so well known, when one starts to brew, most hosts don't give us a second look as we are scooting out the door absurdly early. It got to the point that all we needed to do was to hint that he might be ready to blow, and the mom of the birthday boy would frantically scamper to get our party favors as fast as possible. Griffin became our get-out-of-jail-free card.

At the risk of further alienating some friends and family, I confess that, we may have over used this little trick in the past and still do on occasion. Apologies to my mom for Passover 2003. I'm sure dessert was delicious. I suppose our cover has been blown, and we might not be able to use Griffin as our excuse to be social misfits anymore, but that doesn't mean there aren't other perks we still use to our advantage.

Aren't They Cute?

Fort Lauderdale, like many cities, has an interactive discovery museum with programs geared toward children. Several years ago we went to the museum and watched a movie about the struggles baby alligators faced trying to make it to adulthood. Ignoring the fact that the baby alligators, if successful, would one day grow up to be mammoth predatory reptiles, the producers of the film were able to paint a very sympathetic portrait of the little critters. Think baby bunnies with scales and long tails, only way cuter.

Whenever a larger predator ate a baby alligator, the audience gasped. Some of the children cried. All were genuinely horrified whenever one of the tiny protagonists bit the dust. Except for Griffin. Griffin guffawed whenever the crowd got silent. When the rest of the kids were sobbing, Griffin was giggling and hooting. We got more than a few odd stares and some outright dirty looks. Happily (for me) Griffin's laughing "forced" us to make an early exit from the movie.

Personally, I saw nothing wrong with Griffin's reaction other than that it was different from what society expects. This was a movie, not real life, and it wasn't like human babies or puppies were getting devoured. It was a wildlife documentary about the realities of carnivorous reptiles growing up in the wetlands. We are conditioned to be sad when we see the demise of the star of a movie, but this was merely the laws of nature being carried out. Death is a part of life. The birds, fish, rodents, and neighborhood pets that would eventually be eaten by these predators several years down the line certainly wouldn't shed a tear for them.

Maybe Griffin just has a better grasp on the finiteness of organic existence than the rest of the audience in attendance that day. Nah. More likely, he just enjoyed watching the tiny gators getting swallowed whole by the big ones. Either way, it's times like those that I wish Griffin was able to tell me what was going on in his head and why exactly he was laughing so hard. The question "Why?" doesn't get answered very often when it comes to Griffin.

They Sell What?

Friends of Big Daddy

When I began blogging, in July 2010, I had no idea how many talented special-needs parent bloggers there were out there. Lynn Hudoba, who wrote the introduction to this book, is one such hilariously funny mommy blogger. She blogs about her daughter, Audrey, and her site is a must-visit destination for anyone who enjoyed this book.

I asked a few of my favorite bloggers, including Lynn, to write a post to be included in this book. Their contributions are strewn throughout.

They come from different walks of life and each has a unique style and perspective. Most are raising kids with special needs. All are phenomenal writers and fellow travelers. Enjoy their stories. Maybe you'll find another blogger you love (almost) as much as Big Daddy.

First up:

You're on the spectrum, Charlie Brown!
By Amanda Broadfoot

I've always felt that TV, like the Force, could be a tool for good or evil. For most parents, a simple analysis of good versus evil should suffice in making sensible TV viewing decisions. But if you have an autistic echolalic child, you also have to answer the question, "What do I want to hear repeated nonstop for the next three months?"

Echolalia is the technical term used to describe the tendency among people with autism to repeat stuff they've heard. While my Billy's functional, or nonecholalic language, is increasing all the time, he still fixates on certain TV shows, movies, or books and peppers all conversation with his favorite lines.

We've gone through a *Nemo* phase, a *Thomas the Tank Engine* phase, and a dark period during which Billy discovered the live-action version of *Alvin and the Chipmunks* and nearly drove us all the way to Crazyville. (You haven't lived until you've been awakened at 4:00 A.M. by the scream, "Alviiiiiiiiiiiiiiiiin!!!!!!!!" over the baby monitor night after night after night.)

By far, the worst offender is Charlie Brown. Billy's love of all things Charlie Brown has survived numerous other mini-obsessions. Long after Paddington and Elmo and Curious George have been discarded, lines from the world's most famous blockhead remain with us.

I had, of course, been aware of Charlie Brown before Billy came along. But thanks to Billy, I am also well versed in some of the lesser known entries into the Peanuts oeuvre: *You're Not Elected, Charlie Brown! You're in the Super Bowl, Charlie Brown! Bon Voyage, Charlie Brown! and Don't Come Back!*

But it wasn't until one afternoon when Billy was bouncing around the house, singing, "Charlie Brown ... Failure Face!" at the top of his lungs that I really started to pay attention to the messed up Peanuts worldview.

"Failure Face?" Is *that* what he said?

Billy doesn't always get it right. He has an incredible memory, but he memorizes what he hears, and sometimes he hears it wrong. "Hark, the Herald Angels Sing!" becomes "Mark, the Feral Danger King," for instance.

But I rewound *A Boy Named Charlie Brown* and found a scene where a bunch of kids surround Charlie Brown and sing a jaunty tune to him about what a failure he is. What kind of kids' entertainment *is* this?

Then I started thinking about it: Charlie Brown spends all his time in the psychiatrist's office. Granted, his psychiatrist is Lucy, but then again, his insurance probably doesn't cover therapy. He's bullied and has problems fitting in socially, and he's terrible at organized sports. Based on the sounds he hears his teacher making, I'd say he has some auditory processing issues. And he never seems to enjoy the holidays. He's on the spectrum. Charlie Brown is on the spectrum.

Based on this new perspective, I saw all the shouts of "blockhead" and "stupid" and "loser" and "failure" in a new light. I also realized that reading Billy social stories about appropriate social behavior while letting him watch a cartoon about a bunch of sociopaths abusing a depressed preschooler might be sending mixed messages.

Despite all the abuse, though, Charlie Brown keeps going. He enters the spelling bee. He goes to the Halloween party and tries to direct the Christmas play. He still signs up for the baseball team every spring. And maybe that's a more important message than the insulting dialog: Sticks and stones may break my bones, but one of these days, I'm gonna kick that football.

You're a good man, Charlie Brown.

Amanda Broadfoot is a Florida-based freelance writer, wife, and mother of a brilliant, autistic preschool son and a precocious toddling southern belle. When she can manage to complete a thought and write it down, she blogs at LifeIsASpectrum.com.

Talents and Oddities

Our Little GPS

Neither of our vehicles is equipped with a navigation system, and we rarely use MapQuest. Once we bring Griffin someplace, he remembers precisely how to get there (and home again). On a recent visit to my parent's home in one of the typical Florida gated communities where every home looks exactly like the other Griffin's talent came in handy.

Despite the claims of some builders in Florida, naming your home models the Roma, Firenze, and Milano does not make them individual masterpieces in the timeless style of Italy. Flipping the floor plan, adding a palm tree or moving a half bath does not make a three-bedroom split plan, cookie-cutter house unique or classic.

Thanks to this overwhelming conformity, when visiting my folks, the only way I determine which driveway to pull into is by the vehicles parked out front. On this trip my dad's new car was sitting in the spacious two-car driveway, so I pulled in beside it, careful to only get a few inches of the right tires on the grass. This was quite a feat since it appears "two-car driveway" must lose something in translation from Italian. After taking a moment to gloat about my driving prowess, and fix the patch of grass I dug up pulling in, we all piled out of the car and headed toward the house.

Except for Griffin. Griffin refused to get out and was repeatedly muttering,

"This is not right. This is not right. This is not right."

In hindsight, he should have been yelling, "You idiots! You idiots! You idiots!"

It seems that, since our last visit, my parent's neighbor, two houses up on Torino Terrace (or Sicily Street or Arezzo Avenue—take your pick) admired my father's new car so much that he bought one just like it. Same color, too. However, since muttering is one of Griffin's favorite pastimes, we didn't pay much attention to him and just figured he would get over it and follow us in. As we rounded the corner and approached the front door, my daughter, seeing unfamiliar garden gnomes, lawn jockeys, and insect figurines, recognized our folly and stopped just short of the entranceway. She innocently shrieked, "This isn't Grammy and Poppy's house!"

Like cockroaches avoiding nuclear Armageddon, the three of us scampered back in the car and backed down the street to Grammy and Poppy's place as if nothing had happened.

I had completely forgotten that my dad's car was in the body shop for repairs. A few days earlier he "accidentally" ran over my mom and crashed into their laundry room door a while trying to pull into the garage. He claims it was a gearshift mix-up that caused the incident. I have my doubts. If Griffin knew how to gloat, he would have. If my dad was a better driver, the whole episode could have been avoided. Why my mom was guiding him into the garage like a runway flagman in the first place is still unclear.

You Were Born on a Sunday

Thanks to his love of school lunch menus, Griffin is able to tell you, from memory, what nutritious options the students at West Glade Middle School had for lunch on, say, October 14, 2004. Unfortunately, this is not too helpful at the blackjack tables or for picking stocks. Actually, come to think of it, that particular talent isn't really useful for anything.

Even though they won't make us a ton of cash in Vegas, Griffin does have some fascinating abilities worth describing. By far, his best and most reliable parlor trick has to do with dates. If you tell him your birth date and year, he is able to calculate (in a split second) the day of the week on which you were born. If he is in the right mood, leap years don't even slow him down. This skill has proved both a blessing and curse, so to speak.

Now that its summer we regularly go to the swimming pool in our community. Off to the side of the main pool area there is a hot tub that is overrun by college students during the summer. Griffin loves the hot tub, and I do not. Thanks to my intense germ phobia, I think of it as a huge Petri dish teeming with every STD known to modern medicine. Griffin views it as his own personal bath where strangers come just for the privilege to talk with him. Since he is a strong swimmer, we let Griffin visit the hot tub by himself.

The other day, while walking back to our car, a group of college kids who we had never seen before started hollering from across the parking lot at Griffin. They were chanting his name and he was beaming and flapping his arms like he was going to take flight. A few of the coeds came over to tell him how cool he was, and that after calling their mothers, they found out he was dead on about the days of the week on which they were born. He was totally accurate on every one. Apparently, Griffin was very popular at the hot tub earlier that day.

Pay Per View Follies

Considering his gross- and fine-motor disabilities it's kind of funny Griffin is our electronic device of choice. In our eyes, nothing that Steve Jobs makes can compete with our G-Pod. While Griffin is our favorite gadget, his electronic apparatus of choice is the TV remote. He works the clicker like a gunslinger spinning a Colt 45 or a Jedi knight wielding a light saber. Griffin can't put on his own socks, but he can navigate the blue screen like a brain surgeon. This contention is clearly supported by our November 2008 statement from Comcast Cable.

Like many Americans, our cable bill is one of our biggest monthly expenditures. With Internet access, phone, and premium channels, our bill approaches $200 every month. However, November's statement was over $600 thanks to all the On Demand Movies and Pay Per View Specials we ordered. The only problem was we did not order any On Demand Movies or Pay Per View Specials, and all the remotes and cable boxes in the house have been locked down with the parental control code.

Our initial position was that the bill must have been erroneous. The statement reflected our "purchase" of such high-brow fare as Howard Stern (some sort of farting special), Wrestle Mania (three times), and numerous movies with boobs, *melons*, or *jugs* in the titles. It was as though someone was having a Russ Meyer film festival in our living room.

I spent the better part of an afternoon trying to convince Mrs. Big Daddy that I was not the culprit and that it must have been a billing error. I don't blame her for being a bit suspicious since I had used the incompetent cable company excuse to cover my tracks in the past. The incompetent credit card company and incompetent phone company are equally ineffectual alibis in our house thanks to overuse.

Anyhow, since it wasn't me or Mrs. Big Daddy, and it couldn't have been the kids since all of the purchases were ordered on a weekday morning when the kids were in school and, besides, the remote was child locked, I prepared to do battle with the evil cable company accounting department.

However, before I called Comcast to spend untold hours languishing in automated voice mail hell, Mrs. Big Daddy and I had an almost simultaneous epiphany. It dawned on us that Griffin might have been home from school with a headache on the day in question. At this point, Mrs. Big Daddy started warming to the idea that I wasn't the culprit. In my quest to clear my name, I began to interrogate Griffin. My cross-examination did not go well.

Me: "Griffin, did you figure out our code for the remote and order grown-up movies from On Demand?"

Griffin: "Me?"

Me: "Yes, you. Did you order shows like *Howard Stern Farts* and *Bodacious Tatas Seven, Eight,* and *Nine* on October 16, 2008?"

Griffin: "I had a headache that day. Westglades Middle School had Mexican pizza for lunch."

Me: "That's nice. But did you purchase *Wrestle Mania* at eleven, eleven oh four, and again at eleven oh five on that morning?"

Griffin: "Me?"

Me: "Yes, you. Did you do something naughty with the remote?

Griffin: "I love you daddy."

Me: "Arrgh. I love you, too. But that doesn't change anything. Do not go to channel one ever again. Do you understand?"

Griffin: "Almost."

Me: "I guess I'm paying six hundred bucks for cable this month. Thanks, Griff."

Griffin: "You're welcome."

After clearing that up, we decided that we needed a more ironclad protection mechanism than the childproof code thing. We made arrangements so that nothing can be ordered On Demand using the remote unless Mrs. Big Daddy speaks directly to a Comcast representative first. I guess they must have some sort of voice recognition system. Give Griffin a couple more months, and he'll probably figure that one out, too. I just wish we could teach him to put his underwear on correctly.

Although our cable system is locked down tighter than Fort Knox, our acquaintances and neighbor's TVs are not quite as secure. On one visit to the home of friends of the family, I overheard our host in her distinctive southern accent telling Griffin:

Family Friend: "Yes, Griffin, you can see our remote control but don't even think about going to channel one or ordering any movies or events. Our remote automatically calls the On Demand police if anyone presses channel one. Do you still want the remote?"

Griffin: "No, thank you."

Family Friend: "I didn't think so. Nice try, sweetie."

Wake Up!

Griffin's anxiety about fire and burglar alarms is well known in these parts. However, one type of alarm that has never been a problem in our house is the one that comes standard on most nightstand clocks. We don't own an alarm clock. There's not a single one in any room in the house. Like a homing pigeon that has an instinctual compass, Griffin apparently was born with a remarkably accurate internal clock.

When going to bed, most people set their alarm knowing that seven or eight hours later they will groggily reach over and hit the snooze button a few times before facing the morning madness. For us, we set our alarm by telling Griffin what time we need to get up. Like a Ritz Carlton wake-up call, he has never missed an assignment. Power outages and daylight savings time never stand in his way. The only downside is that there is no snooze button on an autistic kid. Once you tell him you need to be up at a certain time, you are committed to rising at that time—no matter what.

While he is as efficient as a Mussolini railroad, the idea of gently rousing us from slumber is something of an art form that Griffin refuses to master. He slips quietly into the room ninja style, yells, "TIME TO WAKE UP!" and then laughs maniacally like the villain in an old Vincent Price movie. For good measure, we sometimes get an incredibly random weather report for a city thousands of miles from us. Thank you, Al Roker for letting Griffin know about the ice storm headed for the northeast later in the week, but this forecast is utterly useless to me at 6:15 A.M. in south Florida.

Some day Griffin is going realize the power he holds over us in the morning. When he does, we will need to buy an actual alarm clock. Recently, he woke us up only to tell us he didn't want to go to school that day. He wasn't sick. He just didn't care for the weather that day and wanted to stay home—preferably in Mommy's closet professing his desire to be a storm chaser.

Had he not awakened us to tell us he wanted to play hooky, we would probably still be sleeping through dismissal. If Griffin or his sister ever wise up to this, I have a feeling we will be on a first name basis with our local truant officer in no time. The principal already has our number on speed dial thanks to the fire drill.

Dance Party

Making my way home from fat camp reminded me how truly awful air travel has become. But it also made me realize how fortunate Mrs. Big Daddy and I are that Griffin travels so well in light of his idiosyncrasies and sensitivities. He actually puts to shame some NT kids in that respect.

As I was waiting to claim my bag at the end of my odyssey, I flashed back to the trip the entire Big Daddy family took to Washington, DC, earlier this summer. Upon our return, at the very baggage carousel I now found myself, we experienced a uniquely Griffin moment.

When the baggage conveyor belt starts, instead of the loud buzzing warning alarm that is employed at most airports I've been to, at the Fort Lauderdale baggage claim area, Reggae music starts to blare as the luggage begins to tumble onto the carousel. I guess the city council thought adding tropical island music would enhance the "vacation experience" for the many tourists who visit south Florida.

At the end of our DC trip, as a robotic/Muzak version of a Bob Marley tune started to play, Griffin jumped up with a huge smile on his face and started to dance as only he knows how. As he flapped and stomped in front of the road-weary travelers, I noticed that, instead of looking at him with puzzlement and a little disdain (as most strangers in public usually do) a few of them were smiling.

Nobody joined in his dance party, and it only lasted a few seconds. But in my mind, the image is permanently ingrained. It's good to be home.

Objection

As you may already know, Griffin's best and most reliable parlor trick, by far, has to do with dates. If you tell him your birth date and year, he can calculate in a split second the day of the week on which you were born. This skill has proved both a blessing and curse, so to speak.

Friends and family members are occasionally taken in by the seemingly innocent inquiries made by our cute little fact finder. Years ago, a relative we will call Barbara made the mistake of playing the birth date game with Griffin. Then, on a recent visit, the dinner conversation turned to (as it usually does when Griffin is at the table) destructive twisters in the Midwest.

Having grown up in Kansas City, Barbara recalled her harrowing experience during the famous tornado of 1977. She casually mentioned that she was twenty-two or twenty-three at the time. Griffin swiftly and adamantly disputed this assertion. He was all over her "error" like me on a pastrami sandwich. Like a defense attorney voicing an objection to perjured testimony, he yelled, in the middle of Ben's Kosher Delicatessen, for all to hear, *"No! No! No! You were not born in 1955! You were born in 1946!"* [1]

---

1   Some of the names and dates in this anecdote have been changed to protect the innocent. By *innocent*, I mean me.

Wet Weather?

Friends of Big Daddy

Autism's Silver Linings

By Jean Winegardner

There are many things that I have had to come to terms with since discovering that my son Jack has autism. I've learned to deal with his educational needs, find ways to help him make friends, and accept the possibility that he may never move out of my home. Amid all of the tears shed and the big questions about the Future, there are some silver linings that I am grateful for each and every day.

Jack is verbal, and I am grateful for that, but he—unlike my other two children—possesses the ability to keep his mouth closed for more than six consecutive seconds. Between my youngest, asking question after question (after question), and my oldest, trying to manipulate me into giving him everything he wants, sometimes it is quite a joy to go sit with Jack as he plays Legos without feeling the need to narrate everything that he is doing.

This is not to say that Jack is quiet. He absolutely isn't. I'm not going to go into his loud stims (burping and snorting come to mind) because they are most definitely not silver linings. What I will laud is Jack's constant, delightful, on-pitch humming. True, that humming is usually a perfect rendition of the theme from Donkey Kong, but I'm hopeful that it might eventually morph into something beautiful—or at least marketable.

Jack also leads me to better myself through his obsessive interest in different subjects. This interest changes every few months, which helps me broaden my horizons. That stretch of time when he wanted to know everything about space and the planets was über-informational. The era of *Thomas the Tank Engine* was less so, although I can tell the difference between Percy and Henry at fifteen paces. I still can't remember whether Neptune or Uranus is closer to the sun, though.

While I'm not going to say that I enjoyed Jack's speech delay, I will admit that I appreciated the whining and lying delay that came with his autism. Unfortunately, at this point, he's pretty close to indistinguishable from his peers.

One of the manifestations of Jack's autism is that he has a fantastic memory. I wonder sometimes if it is photographic. I don't know if it is, but what I do know is that if Jack is with me, I don't have to remember on which level I parked because he will.

The very best silver lining of all, however, is Jack himself. He is a delightful, loving child who has the ability to feel very deeply and to share those feelings and his love with those he cares about. Namely, me.

(Unfortunately, he doesn't want to share that love with my husband, even going so far as to say tell him, "Your and mom's love can never be." That made my husband vaguely uneasy.)

Jack is hilarious, sometimes on purpose, sometimes not, but always endearing. Of all the silver linings in my life, Jack is one of the brightest.

This said, Jack is seven years old. It is entirely possible that in a few years the ravages of puberty will eradicate all the lovely side effects I've mentioned here. However, I'm hopeful that other new and wonderful things will arrive in their wake, showing me more of the wonder of Jack and the silver linings of autism.

Jean Winegardner, known online as Stimey, believes rodents are funny, autism may be different than you think, and that if you have a choice between laughing and crying, you should always try to laugh—although sometimes you may have to do both. Her personal blog, Stimeyland, can be found at www.stimeyland.com.

Meltdowns

Nuclear Meltdown

Griffin melted down at the mall the other day. Nothing new to see here folks. Keep moving. Only this meltdown had a few new and, in a gallows humor sort of way, funny wrinkles. Yes, we have learned to laugh at even the nastiest of tantrums.

This particular sh*t fit was caused by…oh who am I kidding? I have no idea what caused it. Anyway, it escalated to the point where he was pushing Mrs. Big Daddy and pulling on her ponytail. A security guard took note of the raucousness. It may be the same one who chased Griffin around the mall during the Great Mall Map Heist of '07.

Upon spotting the security guard, Griffin became worried that he would be arrested. This from a kid whose worst defiant act committed in his thirteen years of life is stomping his feet and yanking on his mommy's hair. He does not watch cop shows on TV, and we had no idea how he learned about the concept of being arrested. When he calmed down a bit, Mrs. Big Daddy asked where he learned about incarceration. He replied, "*Bold and the Beautiful.*"

Apparently he has been watching old episodes of the soap on YouTube. Thanks, Ridge Forester.

His punishment for the tantrum was not lawful detainment. Rather he was banned from elevator videos and the weather channel for the rest of the day. Upon the grounding he, as usual, became very apologetic. He begins saying he is sorry whenever he is grounded. When we ask him what he is sorry about, it almost always is that he has lost some privilege but never for the act that earned the punishment.

Today was different. When we asked him what he was sorry about, he didn't immediately blurt out how sad he is for losing his hobbies for the day. Sometimes we need to give him a multiple-choice type of option. He always chooses wrong. But today the oral exam went like this:

Griffin: "I sorry. I sorry."

Mrs. Big Daddy: "What are you sorry about?"

Griffin: "I sorry."

Mrs. Big Daddy: "Are you sorry for throwing a tantrum or are you sorry you can't play on the computer?"

Griffin: "Both. I was a little crazy at Sears today."

We call that progress!

Chuck E Cheese and Me

Chuck E Cheese and I have never gotten along. Our problems go much deeper than the bowel issues eating at this God forsaken place has caused me over the years. The bad blood between us goes all the way back to the late '80s.

For some reason that escapes me all these years later, a few college buddies and me decided to go for dinner at Chuck E Cheese after spending most the day at a local watering hole. Dressed in our acid-washed jeans with strategically ripped T-shirts, we feathered our hair and prepared to play some stupid games and eat some terrible pizza.

One thing led to another, as it usually does after spending six hours in a bar, and before I knew it, I was being viciously assaulted by a six-foot demon rat known as Chuck E. When I went to fight back, I was none-too-gently escorted out of the hellhole. I didn't go back because of the court order until I had kids a decade or so later.

Griffin has never been much of a climber. Actually, when it comes to physical activities, Griffin only really excels at lying around. A chip off the old block. So when we would visit the local Chuck E Cheese Emporium of nightmares when he was six or seven, we never gave much thought to the tubes that run along the ceiling of the place. Like over-sized hamsters, the "typical" kids climb up into this Rube Goldberg contraption and taunt their parents below.

Lil Sis wandered tube city like a gerbil on uppers from the first time we took her. But Griffin stayed away. Until one day he didn't. We only learned of his little exploration into the tubes when Lil Sis alerted us to him melting down inside. She was unable to talk him down. Since I was there solo, I couldn't delegate this disaster to Mrs. Big Daddy.

When I assessed the situation, I saw Griffin's purple tinted face smashed up against one of the highest tubes in the monstrosity. Even muffled by the roar of the other little monsters and an inch of plexiglass, I could see the meltdown was epic in scale.

My options were limited. I toyed with the idea of putting on Lil Sis' shoes, walking out the door and playing dumb when I got home, and Mrs. BD asked what happen to my male progeny. I could try shaking the tubes violently until the boy fell out. Or, I could bite the bullet and climb in there.

Claustrophobia be damned, off came the shoes and in I went. I won't bore you with the gory details, but if you want an idea of how the rescue operation must have looked to those on the ground, think about the sausage making process—only tighter, greasier, and much grosser.

Thanks Chuck E!

The Melodrama

Griffin had, yet another, meltdown at the mall last week. Yup. Again. Nothing unusual about that. It's unfortunate that he hates the mall so much since that's where the elevators are. So if he wants to ride, he needs to put up with the mall.

This tantrum was a big one and, as a punishment, Mrs. Big Daddy told him we were done riding elevators for a while. He was heartbroken. But it didn't stop him from continuing the tantrum on the car ride home and into his room where he hid out for an hour to avoid making contact with me.

When he finally came out of his room, eyes and cheeks all puffy and red from crying, he asked me melodramatically, "Daddy, can I still have elevators in my life?"

How could I say no to that? I do, however, think he is watching way too many soap operas on YouTube.

Bloodletting in the Barbershop

Carl, Griffin's barber, has learned that special accommodations work well for all involved when Griffin sits in his chair. He works the ears as fast as Edward Scissorhands and makes sure the whole buzz cut is done in less than five minutes. We weren't always so lucky to have Carl. Until Griffin was around three or four or five, we used to visit a children's haircutter in the mall.

The blaring Barney videos, computer games, and abundance of toys probably distract typical kids just long enough to get the haircut done relatively painlessly. Unfortunately, the sensory overload didn't work so well for Griffin. Nevertheless, every two months or so, we made a trip to the mall for an hour of torture. The battle plan was as follows.

We would all dress comfortably as though we were going to the gym to workout. A spare shirt would be packed for Griffin since he adamantly refused to be covered in the cape so he inevitably wound up covered in hair, puke, and Big Daddy's tears. When it was our turn, Mrs. Big Daddy would sit in the chair, and I would position Griffin in her lap. She would hold down his arms and torso. My job was neck and head control. It wasn't perfect, but it usually worked well if the stylist clipped quickly and was able to dodge the flailing legs.

On one particular expedition, things did not go smoothly. The hairstylist did not heed our warning about touching Griffin's ears. We specifically told her that *futzing* too much with the ears makes him angry. We told her not to make him angry. She wouldn't want to see him angry. The stylist was not very quick with the ears, and we watched in horror as our little David Banner transformed into the Incredible Hulk. She was totally unprepared for the thrashing, screaming, sweating, and puking. And that was just my reaction!

Lil Sis, who was probably under a year at the time, was not familiar with the hair-cutting process and thought, justifiably from all the commotion, that the hairdresser was hurting her big brother. While we were preoccupied with restraining Griffin, Lil Sis escaped her stroller and bit the hairdresser on the ankle. Thankfully, she did not yet have a full set of teeth so the wound was superficial. However, the bite was the last straw.

The stylist threw in the towel and from her screams of "No mas! No mas!" we surmised the haircut was over, even though it was a bit Three Stoogish. Griffin did not have much language at the time, but he had mastered a few phrases. He turned to the haggard hairdresser, with clumps of his wet red hair still stuck to his face and meekly said, *"Thank you."*

The stylist couldn't help but smile. The $50 tip probably didn't hurt either.

The Answer

Could it really be that easy? After over a decade of inconsolable crying and thousands of tantrums, could it really be that easy? Could there actually be a four-word phrase that shuts down Griffin's meltdowns before they erupt? Nope. But there were about two hours where we had a glimmer of hope. Not really even a glimmer. What's smaller than a glimmer? Whatever it was, it vanished just as quickly as it had appeared.

A few days ago, Griffin's teacher saw a tantrum brewing. If you know the signs, you can usually see one coming, but, like a hurricane, there is nothing you can do to stop it. Once the bottom lip starts quivering, the eyes glaze over, and the tears start flowing, a category five meltdown is not far behind. When it starts, we just try to make it as livable as possible. Like putting on the hurricane shutters and stocking up on bottled water as the storm clouds start rolling in.

This time, it was different. When the tears began streaming down his cheeks, Griffin's teacher simply, and calmly, said to him, "I have no tissues."

And, like the sea parting in front of Moses all those years ago, the crying stopped, and the tantrum was averted. Just like that.

When his teacher relayed this story to us at the end of the day, our first thought was, "Griffin doesn't use tissues.

Ever." Our second thought was, "I have no tissues? That worked? Really?"

We have no idea why this phrase put a plug in the tantrum gusher that was about to blow earlier in the day. But stuff like this no longer surprises us about the boy. We were fairly certain it was a fluke and would never work again, but desperate times call for desperate measures. So we agreed to try it during the next premeltdown cry-a-thon.

We didn't have to wait long. Later that day the cable went out causing Griffin's computer to crash. As the tantrum started revving up, I could hear Mrs. BD frantically yelling from his room,

"I have no tissues! I have no tissues! I have no tissues! I have no tissues! I have no tissues!"

In case you were wondering, it didn't work.

Me So Calm

Griffin has added a new wrinkle to his temper tantrums. He still stomps around, pulls on Mrs. Big Daddy's ponytail, and sometimes cries relentlessly during his sh*t fits. But now he also yells in a voice reminiscent of Lou Ferrigno in the Hulk TV series and Linda Blair in *The Exorcist*. Add to this the fact that, on his best days, his syntax, pronunciation, and diction remind me of Tarzan and you have one comical nuclear meltdown.

During a typical tantrum, in this other worldly voice, he will say things like:

"I AM GOOD BOY!"

or

"I AM CALM!"

Mrs. Big Daddy and I can't look at each other when the Hulk/Exorcist/Tarzan voice comes out or else we will start laughing hysterically. Discipline is difficult when you are giggling like a nine-year-old at your angry autistic son.

Making the scene even more comedic, for some reason, thanks to watching old episodes of *The Bold & the Beautiful* on the Internet, he thinks he can get arrested for throwing these tantrums. This, despite the fact that, as far as I know Stephanie Forester has never vomited pea soup and Bill Spencer doesn't turn green when he is mad. Although, now that I think of it, Ridge and Tarzan could be long lost doppelgangers.

Irrespective, we decided it was a good idea to put an end to Griffin's soap opera addiction. When Mrs. BD broke the news to him he was mildly disappointed.

Mrs. BD: "You are not allowed to watch *Bold & the Beautiful* until you are older."

Griffin: "How old?"

Mrs. BD: "When you are twenty-one you can watch it all you want."

Griffin: "Oooooooh. But, but, but, I will be working at the Weather Channel when I am twenty-one. How can I watch when I am working?"

Apparently he has never heard of long lunches and DVRs. I wonder if the Weather Channel is looking for on air personalities who do an amazing Hulk/Exorcist/Tarzan imitation.

Friends of Big Daddy

HRH Goes Wireless

By Jen

My son was diagnosed with autism at twenty-three months; he is now three years old. When we began our autism journey I never imagined there would be surreal moments that would cause spluttering belly laughter. Case in point is HRH's wireless hotspot.

He started at his ASD preschool this week. His biggest reinforcer is YouTube on his iTouch, and we could hardly send him to his new school without his best reinforcer. I put my thinking cap on and was feeling very satisfied with myself when I solved our problem by buying him his own wireless hotspot. Having his own mobile Internet connection would mean he could have his iTouch and watch film credits on YouTube to his heart's content. Yes, HRH loves to watch the credits that run at the end of a film. Doesn't every three-year-old?

In the shop I was discussing my requirements with a very handsome young man. The hotspot had to be *pay as you go* so that he would have a download limit and I wouldn't get hit with a massive bill at the end of the month. With prepay I had more control. The shop assistant and I were working out the finer details, making sure that the package we were looking at would meet our needs. He asked a few questions, and then I dropped the beautiful phrase "It's okay. It's for my three-year-old."

You should have seen his face! It was only then I realised how strange it must seem for a three-year-old to have his own personal Internet connection. It was one of those surreal moments when I realised that our lives are different and not many three year olds would have their own hotspot. I laughed so much I couldn't talk. He did too. After we composed ourselves I explained about autism and reinforcers. He knows two little boys with autism, and we had a lovely conversation about it.

It is an event I won't soon forget, and I still laugh when I am packing HRH's school bag in the mornings. It also reminded me that "normal" is just a matter of perspective and my "normal" is great.

Jen is the mum of three great children, one of whom has autism. Wife, taxi service, blogger, Internet addict, head cook, and chief bottle washer in her *spare* time, she loves anything tech and spends many happy hours tweaking the html on her blog, http://www.thekingandeye.com/. She works part time for Irish Autism Action as their *Web girl.*

Questions? You Bet!

Statement

Griffin asks a lot of questions. Most of them revolve around elevator videos, *Bold and the Beautiful* characters, Wilford Brimley, and the weather. Usually, by early afternoon, Mrs. Big Daddy and I are worn down by what feels like a marathon *Law and Order*-style interrogation.

At that point we will implement a no-questions rule for an hour. Inevitably, as soon as we announce that the rule is in effect, Griffin's hand goes up as if he were in the classroom. The following is typical of what usually transpires:

Me: "This better not be a question, Griffin."

Griffin: "No, no, no. I have a statement."

Me: "Okay. What's your statement?"

Griffin: "Do you like Bill Spencer from *Bold and the Beautiful*?"

Me: "Ugh."

Shush

Have I mentioned that Griffin asks a lot of questions? He does. On the way to school the other morning was no exception. As I was driving him, still in my PJs and wiping sleep out of the corner of my eye, he was firing them off in rapid succession.

"Why you talk to Jackie on the phone on June 30, 2009?"

"Were you busy in 2009?"

"Busier than in 2010?"

"Why you talk to Jason on the phone on October 30, 2009?"

"Are the lights going to stay on in the house? Why did they go off on November 9, 2009?"

"Do you like my sister?"

"Why you talk on the phone a lot in 2009?"

I fielded these questions and dozens more like them before we even pulled out of the driveway. Halfway to school I was spent and told him to zip it. Actually, I said "Ssshhh!" And this is how the next few minutes of my life went:

Griffin: "Why you say 'Ssshhh'?"

Me: "Enough already with the questions. I don't want to talk about the telephone."

Griffin: "But, but, but you were on the phone a lot in 2009."

Me: "Ugh. I don't want talk about the telephone or 2009 or anything. Let's just have a little quiet for the next two minutes or so. Please."

-Five Second Pause-

Griffin: "Daddy?"

Me: "What now Griff?"

Griffin: "2008."

Me: "Ugghhh!"

Snack or Die

Both Big Daddy and Griffin could stand to miss a meal or two. Yet Griffin is convinced that skipping snack time or moving dinner back by a few minutes may be fatal.

Whenever denied a bag of Doritos or told we will not be dining early-bird style, he will typically ask/plead, "I will not die?"

Someone, somewhere along the way must have mentioned to him that people need nourishment to survive. I am not sure how he made the leap that this means he must snack or die. No matter how much we convince him waiting an hour or two to eat is not fatal, he always seems to have this concern. Either that or he is just playing us for carbohydrates.

Forecasting the After Life

The other evening Griffin asked me "Do people watch Weather Channel when they die?"

Griffin's love of TWC is well known, and we have, on occasion, spoken with him about death. However, this was a strange combination that needed to be answered with wisdom and finesse. Unfortunately, I was the only parent around for the assignment. My inner lazy slob told to me to just answer him with a simple, "No. People do not watch Weather Channel when they die."

Another part of me was screaming to be a good parent and give a thoughtful response that would answer the question but not upset the boy and also be truthful and appropriate for his age and communication capabilities. Unfortunately, I went with the lazy slob response which led to this chat:

Me: "No. People do not watch Weather Channel when they die."

Griffin: "Why?"

Me: "Because dying is sort of like going to sleep, and you can't watch TV while you are asleep."

-Pause-

Griffin: "Can I be awake when I die?"

Me: "I, um…no. When people die, it is more like sleeping, and, besides, I don't want you to think about dying."

Griffin: "If I eat, I will not die?"

Me: "Griffin you're not going to die. Just go to bed. It's getting late."

Griffin: "Can I watch the Weather Channel when I go to sleep tonight?"

Me: "Yes, Griffin."

Griffin: "When I die?"

Me: "Argh."

I'm Not Al

Have I ever told you that Griffin asks a lot of questions? An awful lot of questions? Actually, he only asks a few questions, but he repeats them. Over and over again. And, like a little Geraldo Rivera, he demands concrete answers to his inquiries. It can be tiring.

Unfortunately, sometimes his questions cannot be answered definitively—like his frequent queries about future weather conditions. These conversations often go a little something like this:

Griffin: "It will not rain tomorrow?"

Me: "I don't know, Griff. Maybe."

Griffin: "Do not say 'maybe.'"

Me: "Well, I just don't know. I hope it doesn't rain tomorrow."

Griffin: "Oooooo. Do not say 'hope!'"

-Pause-

Griffin: "Daddy?"

Me: "What, Griff?"

Griffin: "It will not rain tomorrow?"

Me: "Arrghh."

The most frustrating part of these exchanges is that Griffin is never more than ten minutes removed from the Weather Channel. He can tell you what the conditions will be in Reykjavik, Iceland, over the weekend, yet he gets upset if I can't give him assurances about our five-day forecast. Sometimes I think he is disappointed his dad isn't Al Roker. A few more of these weather conversations, and he might even settle for Willard Scott.

Who Knew Car Insurance Was Such a Riot

I'm sure I mentioned this before, but Griffin asks a lot of questions, and he can be quite literal. This combination leads to plenty of material for this blog. Our recent conversation on the way to speech therapy is fairly indicative of this.

His burgeoning interest in Dennis, the Allstate Insurance spokesman, seems to have sparked the following chat:

Griffin: "Daddy."

Me: "Yes, Griff?"

Griffin: "Are you in good hands?"

I was pretty sure he wasn't getting all metaphysical on me and asking if I trust in an omnipotent God to take care of me. I was relatively certain this line of questioning was more insurance related than theological.

Me: "Do you want to know if I have Allstate?"

Griffin: "Yes. Are you in good hands?"

Me: "Nope. Our car insurance is with GEICO. You know, the commercials with the little lizard."

-Pause-

Griffin: "What is car insurance?"

Me: "Well…when you have a car…"

Before I could finish my thought Griffin started giggling hysterically. It wasn't his stimming manic laugh. Rather, it was his this is really funny laugh.

Me: "What is so funny?"

Griff: "You said I have a car!"

Me: "Huh?"

Griffin: "You said 'when you have a car.' I do not have a car. I cannot drive."

This, to Griffin, was the funniest joke he heard all month. I didn't even try to explain any further. He was still chuckling as we walked into the therapist's office.

How Is My Sleep

Friends of Big Daddy

Take That
By Claire Roy

At six years of age, my daughter suffered a brain stem stroke that caused massive brain damage and left her severely physically disabled as well. She did manage to retain some vestiges of her former self, however, in that she could still talk a bit, use her right hand, read, and write and spell at about a grade-one level. She also remembered all her numerals from one to one thousand.

Over the years, we have had many caregivers come and go, some speaking languages other than English. By some miracle, and in spite of her stroke damage, my daughter had the ability to learn new languages easily. So, I taught my daughter many French words and encouraged the caregivers with second language skills to do the same in their mother tongue.

At fourteen years of age my daughter was clearly on par with her peers in the smart-ass department if not academically. She was a first-class user of the magical F-word, and frequently hurled, in sweet, high-pitched tones, that most demeaning of insults: "You are a potato chip!" In spite of the severity of her disabilities, she still had a surprising way of putting people in their place.

That year for a few months, we were "blessed" with a caregiver who could not, for the life of her, stop treating my gal like she was a two-year-old. Her approach would have shamed a kindergarten teacher. She insisted on using this insipid tone of voice and constantly asked my child questions that were more appropriately used in training a chimp. The woman drove us all nuts as we were forced to listen to her coo and gurgle at my teenage daughter, but there was a desperate shortage of help, and we were not keen on abandoning her right off the bat. We repeatedly reminded the woman that my daughter was a teen, and of her limited but very real academic capabilities, but to no avail.

One day, the caregiver asked my daughter yet again in a tone that made the Romper Room hostess sound like a PhD, "Sophie, can you say the alphabet?" At that point, my daughter, clearly fed up, took the bull by the horns and repeated the entire list in French. The caregiver, slightly taken aback, then asked, "Sophie, can you count to three?" I could only imagine the eye roll my daughter would have done if she could have, as well as the resounding *duh* that must have been ringing in her brain. She proceeded to count to ten, this time in German.

We "released" the woman from her duties right after that.

Claire Roy is "just a mom" of two girls, blogger, disability advocate, and former Montessori teacher, caring full time for Sophie up in the Great White North.

The Genie Has Left the Bottle

How Do You Turn this Thing Off?

Marcel Marceau once warned, "Never get a mime talking. He won't stop." The same was true for Griffin. Once he started to speak, we were off to the races—literally and figuratively.

At times, Griffin talks a mile a minute like an auctioneer, at other times he sounds like a borscht-belt Catskills-trained comic, and at other times he just grunts like a caveman. He says things like, "Oy. My knees hurt," when walking the mall, or "I so sweaty," on a humid Florida day. When riding in a crowded elevator he may blurt, "It smells in here."

Hearing a little kid talk like Jackie Mason with no on-off switch and for whom transitions and segues are completely foreign is funny to us. While it may not translate well to the written word, his views on the world around him and his responses to questions leave us baffled and wonder what goes on under that mop of red hair.

Griffin Takes The Cake

Griffin often picks up on sarcasm and understands the concept of a joke, but sometimes his lack of insight results in some unusual conversations like the one I had with him at his eleventh birthday party.

Because of his fascination with all things weather related, we created a custom cake for Griffin, the top of which was made to look like a five-day forecast you would see on the Weather Channel. I had to design, from my imagination, the highs and lows and current conditions since the cake needed to be baked and decorated several days in advance. The forecast, which was beautifully portrayed on the top of the cake, was complete fiction.

In typical Griffin fashion, his first comment upon seeing the cake was that the high for the day was off by several degrees and the low wasn't even close. He wasn't upset about it. He actually loved the concept of the cake. The discrepancy was just something he needed to address. Instead of admiring the cake first and then later joke about the trivial discrepancy, he had to immediately and publicly point it out. He does not always pick up on the nuances of everyday life that are innately obvious to virtually everyone else.

It is probably clear to most kids, even those considerably younger than Griffin, that the point of the birthday cake was not the forecast accuracy. It was the concept of the cake that was important. The fact that this was not how Griffin perceived it is bittersweet for us.

It is this inability to pick up on social clues and abstract concepts that may keep Griffin from ever leading a life that is completely independent of his parents. Statistically speaking, the odds of him achieving a high level of independence as an adult are slim. Oddly, accepting this possibility has had a profoundly positive effect on our life. Now, instead of spending every waking minute trying to "fix" him, we focus on enjoying every moment with him. For the first few years of his life we were so obsessed with curing him that we probably missed out on so much.

Now that we accept Griffin unconditionally, life is infinitely better for all of us. The fact is we feel that we are so incredibly fortunate that we may get to spend all of our years with someone who is so unique and sees the world in a way that no one else does. Of course, everyone has his or her own individual take on the world. Griffin's perspective seems, at times, to be in a league of its own.

Bobby?

Griffin refuses to be called by nicknames. Sure, shortening of his name to Griff or Griffey are okay, and he allows me to call him Tiger and Buddy as I have since he was real little. But new ones are off limits. He balked when a family friend tried to christen him G-Dawg a few weeks ago, and we know better than to call him Dude or Boy.

The other day he asked me a question to which the answer was clearly affirmative so I responded to him with an enthusiastic, "Yesireebobby!"

His protest was swift and decisive, "Do not call me Bobby!" Have I mentioned that he is kind of literal?

Get Out of Town

We have to be careful when using common clichés that most people take for granted. Griffin takes them way too literally. A few weeks ago, when Griffin was acting particularly silly, Mrs. Big Daddy jokingly said to him, "Get out of town!" Griffin's mood changed from playful to crestfallen in a heartbeat as he replied, "I do not want to get out of town. I like this town. I do not want to move again."

I Give You Joke

The occasional misunderstood cliché aside, Griffin actually has a good sense of humor in light of his language and communication shortcomings. However, as any genuinely funny person will tell you, having a good sense of humor doesn't mean you can tell a funny joke. Getting a joke and telling one are two very different things. This is certainly true with Griffin. Griffin's idea of a killer one liner usually goes something like this:

"Daddy, I give you a joke."

Getting ready to fake a guffaw, I tell him to go ahead and hit me with it.

Sounding more like Yakov Smirnoff than Jay Leno he giggles as he says, "You were on the phone with your friend yesterday."

His enthusiastic delivery is great. However, Griffin's material leaves much to be desired. At least he doesn't work blue.

Speedy Checkout

Conversation with Griff while standing in line behind Spanish speaking customers with way over twenty items in the speedy checkout lane at Wal-Mart:

Griff: (Listening to their conversation in Spanish) "Ooooh. That is a lot of noise, Daddy. It sounds like oy oy oy oy oy oy oy oy oy oy oy oy oy oy."

Me: "Sssh!"

Griff: "Why you say sssh, Daddy?"

Me: "Sssh!"

Griff: "Oy oy oy oy oy oy oy oy oy oy oy oy oy oy."

Me: "Sssh!"

Griff: "Why you say sssh, Daddy?"

Griff: "Oy oy oy oy oy oy oy."

Me: "Sssh!"

Griff: "Why you say sssh, Daddy?"

Me: "Ugh."

Three seconds of silence followed by:

Griff: (For all to hear) "Are you mad that these people are making so much noise and taking so long in the line at Wal-Mart?"

HD

Griffin doesn't really watch TV. Unless you count the Weather Channel. If you count TWC, then Griffin watches a lot of television. At times, his room is like a weather center with TWC, tornado videos on YouTube, and his various *Farmer's Almanac*s dominating his little corner of the world. But he never watches cartoons, sitcoms, or movies. It's all weather all the time.

Although he has no interest in TV shows or movies, he sometimes expresses interest in what others are watching. However, by "expressing interest," I really mean asking really bizarre questions. As an example, I give you his conversation several months ago with Mrs. Big Daddy about color versus black and white. Mrs. Big Daddy was watching an old movie when Griffin plopped down on the couch and…

Griffin: "Are you watching a movie?"

Mrs. BD: "Yes. Do you want to watch it with me?"

Griffin: "No, no, no… What year was it?

Mrs. BD: "Nineteen forty-six, I think."

-Pause-

Griffin: "They did not have orange in nineteen forty-six?"

We never did figure out whether he thought the world was black and white back then, or he was able to grasp the concept that it was a limitation in film making technology. We suspect the former because he spent a few days mildly concerned that our world may revert to black and white in

2011. Seriously. He asked for reassurance more than a few times that we would all remain in color.

A few nights ago, while his mom was watching an old film, they embarked on a similar exchange. However, in what must be a sign of the times, it ended differently.

Griffin: "They did not have color in nineteen thirty-nine?"

Mrs. BD: "They didn't have color movies back then, but the world was just as colorful as it is now."

Griffin: "HD?"

Mrs. BD: "No. They didn't have HD back in the thirties."

Griffin: (slightly alarmed): "I like HD. I want to stay in HD. We will still be in color in two thousand eleven?"

Mrs. BD: "Yes, the world will still be in color next year."

Griffin: "HD?"

I cannot wait until the boy catches us watching a 3-D movie. Even better, a 1950s black and white, 3-D flick about the future. That'll rock his world.

John Adams Rocks

Raising an autistic child is challenging. Sometimes it can be overwhelming. Living with Griffin is never predictable. Every day brings us something unexpected.

Case in point: when once asked who his favorite president is, Griffin, without hesitation remarked, "John Adams." After he'd rattled off his birth date, term in office, and party affiliation, I asked Griffin why Mr. Adams was his favorite. Without hesitation, Griffin replied, "Because he is beautiful." I am reasonably certain that no history book has ever described our second president as physically attractive. Mrs. Adams probably didn't even consider her mate handsome. However, Griffin must see the inner beauty in that founding father that George Washington once referred to as "his Rotundity."

The Farting Continues

Friends of Big Daddy

Hello, Shamu!

By Cheryl D

My seven-year-old daughter has Asperger's, a high-functioning form of autism. We didn't get her diagnosed until she was four and a half years old because this form of autism can be harder to detect. There are no major red flags such as a speech delay. In fact, preschoolers with Asperger's can have very advanced vocabulary. In my daughter's case, the obvious red flags were her inability to handle transitions well or anything else that did not go her way.

One thing we thought she did really well was play creatively. She would constantly pretend to be characters she saw on television or people she saw in real life. This was pretty constant. She would get angry if we dared call her by her actual name. It wasn't until my daughter was diagnosed that we found out that what she was doing was called scripting. It wasn't playing creatively at all. She was just recreating things she saw or read about. Nevertheless, the things she scripted were pretty funny at times.

When I started potty training her at three, we were off to a very slow start. One time, she had a huge pee accident on our kitchen floor. She started jumping up and down in her puddle yelling, "I'm a rain cloud!" I found this less cute and funny at the time. Now, I find it hilarious. Disgusting, but hilarious!

Around the same time as the rain cloud incident, we took a trip to San Diego and went to Sea World. My daughter loved seeing the killer whales and dolphins there. She pretended to be them for weeks afterward! Not long after our trip, we were invited to a friend's birthday party. That day, she decided to do something new and pretended to be Shamu's trainer. When we arrived at the party, she went up to her friend's mom and said, "Hello, Shamu!" The mom was a very good sport about it!

One of the strangest things my daughter ever scripted was pretending she was Lou Ferrigno. She had seen an old episode of *Mr. Rogers' Neighborhood* when Lou Ferrigno was visiting and showed Mr. Rogers the process of having his makeup done to look like the Incredible Hulk. While his makeup was being applied, he just sat in a chair. For some reason, when my daughter was sitting on the potty, waiting to go, she yelled out, "I'm Lou Ferrigno!" I don't know if she thought he was on the potty while he was having his makeup done. I didn't bother to ask. I was a little scared about what the answer would be!

Cheryl D. shares her hilarious exploits of raising her daughter with high-function autism at http://littlebitquirky. blogspot.com. She likes to spend her free time, such as it is, reading other blogs, cooking, and watching television.

Hobbies a/k/a Obsessions

Hurricane Season

We are in the heart of hurricane season here in the southeast, and Griffin is doing remarkably well compared to years past. Griffin's infatuation with the weather started in 2004 or 2005, when we had incredibly active storm seasons. His fear of thunderstorms has been intense ever since. Desperate for anything to ease his anxiety, we thought, if he could see weather reports and know what's coming, Griffin's storm-related angst would be somewhat allayed. So, we introduced him to the Weather Channel.

It wasn't long before Griffin became a weather junkie. Sometimes, while surfing the Web in search of old tornado footage, Griffin keeps the Weather Channel blaring in the background. It's like he has his own weather command center. The National Hurricane Center has nothing on him.

Being constantly tuned into the weather has done absolutely nothing for his trepidation of thunderstorms, but it does give him something to talk to his friends and family about. Obsessively. When he chitchats about the local conditions, it is not idle small talk. He takes his conversations about the weather much more seriously than most. He considers Nick Walker a close friend, and he always wakes up with Al.

Nevertheless, Griffin's dream of a career as a meteorologist is probably not going to be fulfilled. Inconsolable crying and quivering in Mrs. Big Daddy's walk-in closet during a mid afternoon shower is not a great quality for a storm chaser. His dash for the closet at the slightest chance of precipitation is so routine that his sister sometimes brings him snacks, his blankets, and books to read during particularly long storms.

The fact we live in the southeast is truly unfortunate for poor Griffin. During hurricane season (which is now officially considered to run from March 1st through February 28th annually, except for leap years) our weather varies from hot and humid, to blistering and muggy, to scorching and stifling. To add insult to injury, there is always a 100 percent chance of afternoon typhoons.

If we let him watch our local weatherman (aka Chicken Little), Griffin would surely convince us to amass a warehouse full of plywood, flashlight batteries, bottled water, sandbags, and canned beans in anticipation of the inevitable "Big One." Our local news has been forecasting the imminent arrival of a category nine storm every week since 1993. The actual local climate coupled with our absurd media hysteria doesn't bode well for a kid who sweats like his dad and is terrified of the rain.

During one squall last summer, Griffin hunkered down in the closet and sobbed about how much he wanted to be storm chaser. When Mrs. Big Daddy calmly explained that storm chasers like Jim Cantore don't hide in the closet when it drizzles, he nearly vomited. I am reasonably certain that crying so hard you puke is not what the Weather Channel is looking for in its on-air personalities.

Wilford

Thanks to Wilford Brimley's TV commercials, Griffin is convinced that anyone over sixty-five is a diabetic and must call Liberty Medical for all their diabetes testing supplies. He is not shy about telling everyone about the benefits of calling Wilford, regardless of their current health status. He has even asked for an advance on his allowance so he can call Liberty Medical and get diabetes supplies delivered right to our door.

For the record, we have no affiliation with Liberty Medical and receive no monetary compensation for Griffin's endorsement. The same is true for AARP, which he happily recommends to everyone, regardless of age. I am only forty-three, and Griffin has been getting me excited for my impending initiation into the AARP fold for several years now.

For a fantasy trip, most kids would want to get a chance to sit in the Yankees' dugout before a game. Griffin would probably prefer to have Mr. Brimley give him a tour of Liberty Mutual's corporate headquarters. Say what you will, but I think we have a much better chance of seeing those cubicles than visiting the famous infield in the Bronx. However, getting Griffin a walk-on role in *Cocoon 3* is probably a long shot.

Recently there have been signs Griffin's unrequited love of Mr. Brimley is waning. He has been talking about someone named Dennis, and he innocently asked me the other day, "Are you in good hands, Daddy?"

Looks like I'll be getting Allstate next time my auto insurance policy expires. Sorry GEICO, the gecko apparently doesn't do it for Griffin.

Believe it or not, his odd talents and even his fascination with aging character actors and AARP bring us much joy. We love the peculiar things that come from Griffin's mind and out of his mouth. Long ago, we stopped trying to "fix" or "cure" Griffin. We don't try to stifle him and make him conform. Now, we accept Griffin as is, with all his idiosyncrasies. Even if it means eventually having to wean him from a nasty addiction to infomercials geared toward the geriatric set.

Even though we address what we can, we realize that, much like you cannot take a toothpick and expect to transform it into a log cabin, we do not look at Griffin and foolishly believe we can make him into super "typical" kid. So be it. He prefers Wilford Brimley and glucose meters to Kobe Bryant and the NBA. It could be worse. He could have seen those Viagra commercials from a few years back and become obsessed with Bob Dole and erectile dysfunction. I don't even want to think about what he would do if he caught those ads featuring Smilin' Bob hawking Enzyte.

Pick a Number

Griffin recently received his autographed picture of Wilford Brimley. This has sparked a renewed interest in Liberty Medical and their diabetes testing supplies. Since you need to be sixty-five or over to participate, Griffin is getting us ready by having us declare at what age we will begin ordering our supplies from Wilford's company. He has now, excitedly, asked each member of our family, "When will you call Liberty Medical? Pick a year between sixty-five and when you die."

I picked age 179.

You're Never Too Old for BJ

What? Oh come on! Get your minds out of the gutter. The BJ I was referring to is Barney's (the singing dinosaur) rambunctious, jaundice, and cheerful dinosaur friend. Really, you guys need to get a hobby or something to keep your heads in the right place. Sometimes I think Griffin isn't the only middle schooler I'm dealing with.

Speaking of Griffin and middle school, it seems he is now curious as to which of his hobbies and interests are age appropriate and which are not. If we were to be completely honest with the boy, we would have to break it to him that some of his interests are not age appropriate and all the others are, well, just alien to most people of any age.

In addition to elevators, elevator videos, the Weather Channel, Wilford Brimley, the *Bold and the Beautiful*, and mall maps, Griffin likes to play with his ABC blocks and (if he were not embarrassed about it) watch *Sesame Street* and Barney. He frequently asks:

"Am I too old to watch Barney?"

"Do middle school kids play with blocks?"

"Why you fart so much, Daddy?"

He is clearly torn. He still enjoys the blocks and, every time he walks by the giant Sesame Street book we got him years ago, he looks at it longingly. We repeatedly tell him it's okay to play with these things. No one at school needs to know about it and, if it makes him happy, why not? As of now, he stills plays with his blocks, and, every now and again I'll catch him watching the Cookie Monster on YouTube.

Love of an Elevator Part One

One of Griffin's greatest passions is riding elevators. No matter how fun we try to make sports seem, Griffin always returns to his true love—elevators. I bet you didn't know there are various sites on the Internet dedicated exclusively to riding elevators. That's right—type in the word *elevator*, and you will find that there are people who travel the world filming themselves riding elevators. More than a few of these folks post their videos on YouTube and get thousands of hits. Little do they know that most of these hits are coming from our playroom.

Several of these elevator aficionados give themselves clever nicknames and get creative with their filmmaking techniques. I am sure none of them has a bigger fan than Griffin. He watches the lift jockeys riding elevators in strip malls, department stores, hotels, office buildings, parking garages, colleges, hospitals, and airports. He talks about his favorite elevator filmmaker's work as if it were as important as Spielberg making *Schindler's List*. It is going to be difficult to break it to Griffin that somehow the academy overlooked Elevator Farts in its Oscar nominations again this year.

Watching videos of elevators is not nearly as satisfying for Griffin as actually riding in them. We make trips to malls, office parks, and tall buildings for the sole purpose of surfing the vertical tube. He emulates the style of his favorite heroes when pushing the buttons and almost always comments on the décor and condition of the elevator car.

On a recent elevator safari to the local megamall, we had to travel through the women's lingerie department in Macy's to get to the elevator. As though he was seeing the bra-clad mannequins for the first time, Griffin exclaimed loudly, "Oooh. Macy's sells boobies!?! Do you believe that?!?"

Upon reaching the elevator, Griffin channeled his inner Captain Elevator and launched into his narration:

"Wow! That was a great hallway. I am now pushing the Up button. Here comes the elevator. Ooh! It is a very nice elevator. It is a General. Time to push the button for the second floor. I am now pressing the door-close button. The door is closing. Here we go. It smells funny in here. Here we come to the second floor. I'm so sweaty. Here we are."

Sometimes we get strange looks and sneers from other passengers who are used to the silence people customarily observe when riding an elevator. But the smile on his face and the pure joy Griffin gets from this simple pleasure is worth every leer and snicker.

I would love to say that the mouth-breathing Neanderthals who judge Griffin without knowing him don't bother us at all, but we are human. By now, we should easily be able to shrug this sort of thing off. Mrs. Big Daddy usually handles the idiots who are visibly taken aback by Griffin's love of elevators by declaring, "It's cheaper than taking him to Disney World!"

Love of an Elevator Part Two

Big Daddy doesn't do stairs. Griffin loves elevators. Perfect match. In the business world they would call this *synergy*. We call it awesome.

Having a child with autism is a challenge. But, on occasion, there are some nice perks. Like the excuse to be lazy and use the elevator even if we are only going up one flight. At times I find myself saying stuff like, "I would love to use the stairs, but my son is autistic and loves to ride elevators. I wouldn't want to disappoint him. Want to ride with us or will we meet you up there?"

I hope my cardiologist doesn't read this.

Love of an Elevator Part 3

I've posted before of Griffin's love of elevators. While it is a cheap hobby, not all our elevator rides have been totally free of charge. We have learned that taller and fancier doesn't always mean better for Griffin. For example, last summer I took the family back to my roots—to the biblical homeland. We took a weeklong vacation to New York City. I left my Long Island birthplace when I went to college at seventeen and never moved back. In my forties, I figured it was time the kids got to see where I grew up. The land of the $18 movie ticket, incomprehensible and unexplainable traffic, jaywalking, and year-round gray skies.

I arranged for all the touristy things like the Museum of Natural History, a Broadway show, a horse and carriage ride through Central Park, getting pickpocketed on Canal Street, and a horrifying taxi ride through midtown during rush hour. For Griffin, I also made sure we stayed in the Marriot Marquis, with its forty-plus story glass enclosed elevator, and I prepurchased VIP tickets (for around $100) to ride the Empire State Building elevator to the observation deck. While he enjoyed the hotel elevator (which was the only thing that came free with the obscenely overpriced "suite"), he was not at all impressed with the Empire State Building. Rather, the highlight of his trip was riding in the midtown Macy's elevator. Go figure.

We love that Griffin is our little Cliff Clavin of Otis-related knowledge and the Sir Ernest Shackleton of elevator expeditions. When we think about the future, we sometimes imagine Griffin being an elevator operator. I think he would be adorable in the little hat and uniform. Plus, he would get to chat about the weather with riders all day long. Talk about job satisfaction.

When I envisioned my life years ago, I never thought I could get so much satisfaction riding elevators with my twelve-year-old son. To borrow a line from the Grateful Dead, what a long strange trip it's been.

Mall Map Mayhem

There was a time when Griffin was into mall maps. We visited malls all over the southeast picking up store directories from information booths at all our stops. Mrs. Big Daddy didn't mind because it almost legitimized her nasty shopping habit. Almost.

One benefit we now have is that, with respect to all the malls within a fifty-mile radius of Casa de Big Daddy, we never have to ask directions to the food court or the Gap. Best of all, there is nothing quite like watching your adorable red-headed kid get admonished by an octogenarian security guard for trying to take all the store directory maps from the information kiosk.

Our local malls no longer put the maps out front. They are safely tucked behind the counter thanks to our little collector.

Grazing

Griffin "played" soccer several years ago in an extra-ordinarily well-intentioned special program where high school kids volunteer to be teamed up with children with disabilities. His buddies were two female sophomores who Griffin quickly manipulated into letting him graze instead of kick. He contentedly sat and ate grass for an hour while his escorts tried to convince him to, at the very least, stand up and pretend to play defense. He wasn't much of a fullback, but if he was a billy goat, we would have been so proud of Griffin's cud and bolus production. I wonder if his volunteer buddies got service credit for their fine work as shepherds.

Griffin's teammates weren't really any more productive. Watching the other buddies assist their assigned autistic children play the world's most popular sport reminded me of trying to juggle greased puppies. Although the game was much more chaotic. If our experience was indicative of America's progress in the sport, Spain has nothing to fear in the next few World Cups!

Regardless, Griffin's disinclination toward the pastime Europeans affectionately call "the beautiful game" was not all that disappointing. Mrs. Big Daddy and I tend to agree with former NFL head coach, Mike Dikta who once said, "If God had wanted man to play soccer, he wouldn't have given us arms." I never could understand the logic behind a sport where risking brain damage by purposely putting your head in the path of a speeding ball is acceptable, but you get severely penalized for even brushing against it with your hands.

Fast-forwarding half a decade: Griffin joined Soccer Buddies again and enjoyed it immensely. Now that he is older and seems to understand the concept of the sport, he actually kicked the ball occasionally, and ran up and down the field. We try not to pay too much attention to the fact that each time he galloped toward the goal he would turn to us on the sidelines and try to make sure that we would be getting him pizza immediately upon conclusion of the game. Whatever motivates him is fine with us.

Like a Hot Potato

Last spring Griffin participated in Soccer Buddies, a program where high school kids volunteer a few hours of their Saturdays to play soccer with children with disabilities. Each kid gets assigned a buddy or two to shadow him or her throughout the practices and "games." Many of the special needs kids (Griffin included) wouldn't be able to participate in organized team sports without a program like this.

Griffin's buddy this past season was a sophomore boy who worked great with him. Let's call him Ryan. Ryan, who has a younger brother on the spectrum, was able to wean Griffin off his nasty grazing habit from years past, and actually got him to run up and down the field kicking the ball in the right direction. Occasionally. Since Griffin loved him, we asked the league coordinator to assign Ryan to Griffin next soccer season.

In the meantime, since the new soccer season is a far way off, we signed Griffin up for Flag Football Buddies. We totally forgot to request his old buddy. But, we rationalized it might not be bad to have a new buddy for this new sport. Change is good for a kid like Griff. Right?

The first football game was last weekend. Griffin was sobbing the whole way to the park about how he missed Ryan and didn't want a new buddy. Upon arrival at the field, we learned Griffin was assigned two new buddies—high school girls. Hmm.

Have I mentioned how much Griffin loves girls? He was, not surprisingly, positively punch drunk over this unexpected turn of events. When we asked him if he wanted us to try and switch him to be paired up with Ryan his response was a swift and emphatic," No, no, no, no, no, no!"

As he took the field with his new and improved buddies, Ryan (who was assigned a different kid for football) spotted Griffin and ran over to say hello. Griffin gave him a half-hearted response before being rustled away by his new cutie buddies. His old buddy didn't seem to mind the hot potato treatment as he turned to us on the sidelines and shrugged before running off to his new charge.

I hope when soccer season comes around Ryan makes Griffin pay for the slight with laps or sit-ups or by forbidding him from talking about Wilford Brimley or elevator videos during the game. Would serve the kid right.

Glass Bottom Boat

Friends of Big Daddy

No Comparison
By Jennifer Bush

In the house where I grew up, there is a fireplace set into a large brick wall. Each holiday season, we would tape all of the holiday cards we received on this wall. I loved checking the mail every day and putting up those cards as they came in. Now that I'm in a house of my own, I carry on the tradition by putting all of our holiday cards on our mantle and watching the collection grow as the New Year approaches.

This year, one card caught my eye, and I kept coming back to look at it. It is the card from a friend of mine whose daughter is just a few months younger than my son. This little girl is feisty and adventurous, and I don't think her mom will mind if I say a little bit of a troublemaker. I adore her.

I couldn't help but think about the scenarios in each photo, and what those would be like if my son, Moe, were in those same situations. I know that as a parent of a special needs child, I'm not supposed to compare. I know it is the opposite of acceptance, an exercise in futility at best. I also know that sometimes it can be really funny.

Holiday Card Scenario One: Girl in bee costume, complete with antennae, eating a cupcake. There are a few crumbs around her mouth.

Our version: Bee antennae are nowhere to be found because Moe refuses to wear them. They were probably being chewed on, but dropped when cupcakes were spotted. Moe has pushed the cupcake in its entirety into his face, the cream filling smashed in between his fingers. His face is completely covered in chocolate, as is the bee costume.

Holiday Card Scenario Two: Girl is riding a pony, wearing a helmet.

Our version: Horseback riding is supposed to be therapeutic for people with autism, so assuming that we could forgo the helmet requirement and get Moe to stop eating mud and actually sit on the horse, he likes it. Until he decides he is done and then suddenly jumps off the horse. Since we're never more than an inch away from Moe when we're out, I'm pretty sure someone catches him.

Holiday Card Scenario Three#3: Girl smiling while sitting on Santa's lap.

Our version: Moe pulls on Santa's beard, bites his arm, and we are asked to leave.

Holiday Card Scenario Four: Girl dipping feet in rushing stream.

Our version: Moe loves it. He is lying down in the freezing cold water, my husband gets soaking wet trying to make sure Moe doesn't drown. I am on the shore with our daughter who is screaming to go in too, when I realize I have brought neither towels nor change of clothes for either child.

Holiday Card Scenario Five: Girl holding and examining frog.

Our version: Moe tries to bite Frog. In the background, I am running, shouting "not for mouth!"

Holiday Card Scenario Six: Little girl snowboarding.

Our version: Three-year-olds can snowboard? It doesn't matter. My family doesn't believe in cold weather, so we would not be outside in the snow.

Our family's adventures may be more of the let's hope Moe doesn't bite the woman cutting his hair variety and less of the outdoor sporting variety, but they are our adventures nonetheless. And the love I have for that little boy, full of pure joy as he shoves a cupcake in his mouth—for that, there is no comparison.

Jennifer Bush lives in the Silicon Valley with her husband and two kids, including a preschooler on the autism spectrum. She has degrees in Sociology and Communications from UC Berkeley and an MBA from Yale. You can find her at her personal blog, Anybody Want A Peanut? www.wantapeanut.com or on Twitter @wantapeaut.

Eeeewwww!

What's That Smell?

I don't blame Huggies and Pampers for assuming that most five-year-olds are either completely potty friendly or at least ready for pull-up training pants and for ignoring the small segment of the market that still need good old-fashioned diapers at this age. However, I do blame the diaper makers for causing me to throw up violently and repeatedly in a Blockbuster parking lot in the early part of this millennium. I wish I had known back then about NASA's maximum absorbency garment (MAG) made famous by astronaut Lisa Nowak on her journey of love from Houston to Orlando.

Griffin has gross- and fine-motor issues that delayed (and still delay) his physical development in many ways. At the time of our Blockbuster outing, even though he was five, he still spent significant time in my arms and/or in the stroller. He also was years away from being potty trained. On this trip, Griffin's little sister got dibs on the stroller, so I had to carry the big feller as we perused the new releases.

Since his first bowel movement, Griffin has always suffered from digestive issues leading to watery stool and, frequently, diarrhea. We have tried all sorts of wheat and gluten-free diets to no avail. Although many parents swear by this holistic approach, we found that these regimens were difficult to maintain, and Griffin did not show any positive results from them.

While strolling the video rental aisles, a strong and pungent odor permeated the air around me. By "strong and pungent" I mean it was clearly a form of biological warfare. It smelled like a blend of WWI mustard gas and a New York City subway car in an August heat wave. Being the mature and loving husband that I am, I immediately yelled for all to hear that my wife just let loose the mother of all farts. Actually I think I hollered, "Gas leak in aisle three!"

Mrs. Big Daddy, as she always does, vehemently denied cutting the cheese. After shooting me a quick "Whoever smelt it, dealt it," retort, we continued browsing for another three seconds until the smell became overwhelming. Watching the paint peel off the wall, other patrons begin to pass out and, and wanting to avoid having to call in a hazmat team, Mrs. Big Daddy decided to do a diaper check.

After one quick peek at Griffin and me, Mrs. Big Daddy cried, "Uh-oh. Let's go. Now!"

It's never a good sign when a woman who has changed thousands of diapers starts to panic in this type of situation. So, without looking down, I followed her out the door and to the car.

When Mrs. Big Daddy peeled Griffin from my arms I was stunned at the carnage. My right arm, shirt, and part of my shorts were covered in a steamy light brown viscous stream of lava. The smell hit me immediately, and I began to dry heave. To say I was of no assistance to Mrs. Big Daddy in the clean-up project is an understatement. I was as helpful as Homer Simpson would have been at Chernobyl.

While Mrs. Big Daddy began her triage and searched for the nearest toxic waste dump site, I started retching like a frat boy on spring break. Mrs. Big Daddy had to do the ultimate in multitasking. She didn't know which of her baby boys to help first. She alternated between getting Griffin out of his diaper and helping me through my own personal crisis.

If there was one bright side to this debacle, it is that I didn't get pulled over driving home in my underwear with a nearly naked five-year-old in the backseat. Another hidden blessing from that night—we avoided wasting $2.50 on *American Pie Two*.

Please Stand Up

A few years ago Griffin and I found ourselves in one of the dirtiest fast food joints to have ever existed this side of Calcutta. It was at this time that Griffin was going through a phase where he insisted on visiting every public restroom he saw. He usually didn't need to use the facilities. Mostly he just wanted to see if it was clean, well decorated, and if it had a window. Unfortunately, sometimes he actually needed to use the bathroom for its intended purpose. It was these "active" excursions that forced me to temporarily abandon my germ phobia and clean off toilet seats for my stubborn son who refused to stand when he pees.

As recently as a few hundred years ago, men wanted male offspring to carry on their name, gain political power, plow their fields, and inherit their kingdoms. The only remaining modern day advantage of having boys is that they stand up when they piddle. For me, this last surviving perk of male progeny has been wiped out by Griffin's insistence on sitting when he urinates.

For those readers of the female persuasion, a brief explanation of the dilemma this poses may be in order. The idea of lifting a seat, flushing, or even aiming at the toilet in a public men's room is as foreign to guys as a unicorn wandering down Forty-Second Street. For that reason, it is only in the most extreme and dire situations in which a man will dare to sit in a public restroom. I have been known to endure intestinal ruptures in an effort to avoid this fate.

A very young boy can accompany his mom, if she is available, or be held over the seat by his father for a contactless deposit in other situations. However, even if the mom is present, bringing an eleven-year-old boy into a women's room is fraught with pitfalls we try to avoid. Even Arnold Schwarzenegger can't hold Griffin's hundred-plus-pound frame over the bowl while the boy chitchats about elevators instead of quickly doing his business.

Because of this, I've cleaned commodes in countless locations, including the New Jersey Turnpike, Canal Street, the Empire State Building, every Florida theme park (more than once), public beaches, and sports arenas.

This particular beauty was beyond cleaning. It was worse than a Porta-Potty after a weekend of Grateful Dead shows. Decorating the seat was not an option. Nothing I could do without a pressure cleaner, a gallon of bleach, and a Sham-Wow would make the throne fit for use. We needed to stand. The urinal was only marginally better, but since Griffin was too short to use the sink and too classy to go on the floor, we had no choice. I helped him pull down his pants and stood behind him waiting for nature to call as Griffin screamed and protested. Since he was eleven or so at the time, the scene must have looked creepy to any other customers who wandered in.

While I was busy holding him up by his torso in a make-shift half nelson, Griffin decided the contents of the urinal needed to be emptied before he deposited his precious cargo in it. So he reached in and pulled out the rubber drain guard, pieces of chewed gum and fermented urinal cake. What little parental instincts I have kicked in, and I grabbed the bounty from Griffin.

Before I knew it, I was the one holding the quickly crumbling and dripping hockey puck-sized urinal mint. In my hands, moments before I was going to indulge in a few Whopper Juniors, was the residue of the excretion of countless BK patrons. As the unmistakable stench of urine, mucus, and stale Juicy Fruit gum surrounded us, I washed our hands furiously. The hand washing continued obsessively like Lady Macbeth, for months to come. Needless to say, I did not eat that afternoon, but Griffin chowed down his double cheese-burger and large fries without a second thought.

In a strange way this episode proved to be a great learning experience for me. Griffin, as he often does, forced me out of my comfort zone. I had to face my germ phobia straight on in the worst sort of way. It was horrifying and disgusting, but I didn't die. I did not get ill. Best of all, I did not mindlessly inhale 1,500 empty calories and 100 grams of saturated fat.

Hanging Out: Booger Edition

Yesterday, Griffin appeared in the doorway to my office/man cave and gleefully said, "Daddy, look at me!" When I looked up I saw he had a big smile and his finger jammed so far up his nose it looked like he was tickling his brain. He knows this is disgusting, and I am almost sure he was doing it to annoy/amuse me. Nonetheless, I am a parent (barely) so I dutifully yelled at him to remove his finger from his nose. The following chat ensued.

Griffin: "But, but, but, but I am not at school."

Me: "It doesn't matter. Picking your nose is still disgusting whether you are at school or at home."

Griffin: "But I am not picking my nose. I am just hanging out."

That boy still really doesn't get the concept of hanging out.

Is That Disgusting?

Since starting middle school, Griffin has been interested (somewhat) in learning what types of behaviors are considered disgusting as opposed to those deemed acceptable by most kids his age. Even though he has no intention of giving up the stimming, flapping, and maniacal laugh, at least we've been able to shame him into resisting the urge to say, for example, fart in public. Mind you, in that respect, Big Daddy does not lead by example. It's more of a "do as I say not as I do" sort of thing.

In the car a few nights back, Griffin and Mrs. Big Daddy engaged in the following discussion:

Griffin: "Is picking your nose disgusting?"

Mrs. BD: "Yes, Griffin. It's gross."

Griffin: "Is it more disgusting than touching your butt?"

Mrs. BD: "I don't know, Griff. They're both pretty disgusting."

Griffin: "But, but, but sometimes my nose is itchy."

Mrs. BD: "I know. That is why we use tissues to blow our nose. You don't see Daddy or Mommy picking their nose, do you?"

At this point in the conversation there was an uncomfortable pause. His answer on this one could go either way. Lil Sis was completely at ease, but Mrs. BD and I were a bit concerned with how much the boy had observed over the years.

I know I may not have always been that, um, proper and discreet in my interior nose scratching when it was just Griff and me in the car. From her silence, I assume Mrs. BD had similar thoughts running through her head. Sometimes, especially when he was younger, we had a tendency to forget that, even though he couldn't communicate well, he was still taking in data. Potentially embarrassing data.

I held my breath a bit until Griffin, somewhat dejectedly, said, "No."

Whew. Dodged a bullet on that one.

Revisiting Lunch

Griffin has thrown up without warning at Sea World, on a glass-bottomed boat, on a horse, in a fireman hat on Halloween, and in virtually every room in our house. Once he actually barfed in a toilet. We call that one the fluke of puke. More often, Griffin has blown chunks on various family members.

When he was a baby, I used to lie on my back on the floor and toss Griffin up in the air. I was told babies love this acrobatic routine, and I was assured it was safe. Besides, Griffin ate this activity up. He has been described as having both hyper- and hyposensitivity, which may explain his fascination with roller coasters, swings, and this type of quasi-gymnastic act.

Griffin is overly sensitive to certain stimuli while completely numb to others. When he was a toddler he could stand on broiling hot paver blocks for hours at a time but used to stiffen up like a corpse when anyone went to hug him. He would listen to the Wiggles repeatedly, but a few seconds of Celine Dion caused bloodcurdling screams. I don't really blame him on that last one.

We retired the Cirque du Soleil act the day Griffin had an out-of-stomach experience on my face. I was wearing glasses that protected my eyes from the molten liquid goo I watched come out of his mouth like a slow motion volcano and splash on my forehead. As the hot liquid dripped down my face toward my nostrils and mouth, my instinct was to stop, drop, and roll.

However, those pesky "parental instincts" that would later make me voluntarily hold other men's urine in a Burger King restroom to protect my son, reminded me that I still had to gently put down the oblivious spewing infant, secure him in his bouncy seat, and walk to the kitchen before I could wipe the mess off my face. Thankfully, Griffin's diet consisted only of soy formula at the time. Others have not been so fortunate.

There Are Easier Ways

Friends of Big Daddy

The Rules
By Laura Hand

It's been pretty well documented that kids with autism are rule followers. This is especially true of our son, Coleman. He has always had a deep-seated need for everyone to follow the rules. This was apparent even before we knew of his diagnosis. I'll never forget the incident I witnessed one day when picking him up from preschool. The carpool lane passed right by the playground, and I arrived early so I could stop a minute to watch my boy play with his classmates. I pulled alongside the fence just as the teacher was calling for the children to line up. Coleman sprinted to the fence and was the first in line, but none of the other children were even beginning to wander over. Coleman gripped the fence so as not to get out of line, leaned forward, and yelled, "IT'S TIME TO LINE UP! IT'S TIME TO LINE UP!"

Not a single child moved. They all just continued with their play because let's face it, who's going to listen to a three-year-old boy gripping a chain link fence for dear life and yelling about lining up? This presented Coleman with a quandary: stay put and follow the rules, despite the increasing anxiety being generated by his rebellious classmates, or break the rules and leave the fence to round up the little hooligans. What happened next was astounding. My son, the sweet little blonde with the Charlie Brown head, left the fence and began chasing after his peers insisting they line up. He looked like a human border collie.

Like all parents, we gave him some of the basic rules of polite conversation—things like saying please, thank you, you're welcome, and God bless you. Once advised of the rules, he would get upset if we didn't adhere to them 100 percent of the time. He'd thank us for something and, if we didn't say, "You're welcome," he would insist that we say it. This didn't just happen occasionally. This happened every single time.

It was frustrating, but eventually we started using this to our advantage. Whenever we need to ensure that he'll obey, we start it with "the rule is." For example, the rule is you don't go into the street. For some reason, simply telling him not to go in the street doesn't make the same impression as putting it in terms of a rule. I can't tell you how glad I am that we employed that tactic.

On the first day of first grade the teacher was discussing the different ways the children got to and from school and said, "and Coleman walks home." Coleman heard that, gathered up his things, and walked straight out of the school. No one noticed. Fortunately, the rule was if he got out the front door, and Mommy's wasn't there, he was to sit on a certain bench and wait, and that's just what he did. At some point, a woman going into the school saw him and took him inside where he returned to class. Some say rules are made to be broken. Thankfully, Coleman doesn't subscribe to such nonsense.

Laura Hand is the married mother of two beautiful children whom she's been homeschooling since 2007. She authors a blog about her family, where each member has an autism spectrum disorder, at Life in the House That Asperger Built at www.lifewithasperger.wordpress.com.

Friends

Hanging Out

Griffin has picked up a new term in middle school—hanging out. Now, every time, I pass by his room or tell him to be quiet, he asks me if we are hanging out. He so badly wants to hang out, but I'm not sure he knows what it is.

My interpretation of hanging out is spending time with someone while doing nothing in particular—kind of like loitering or waiting for a pizza. Fielding a barrage of questions about Wilford Brimley or elevator videos is not hanging out. That is a press conference or a police interrogation.

Irrespective, Griffin wants to hang out with his friends from middle school. There is one eighth grader in particular he wants to hang with. I'll call him Ethan. From what we can decipher, Ethan is only in Griffin's class part of the day. Our guess is that he is not autistic but requires some extra help in speech or for antisocial behaviors.

Just because Griffin speaks about him everyday does not necessarily mean that Ethan has any idea who Griffin is. In the past Griffin has established friendships with Jim Cantore (the Weather Channel), Wilford Brimley (beloved character actor), and Bill Spencer (ruthless magazine magnate on B&B). So we don't know if Griffin has ever really talked to Ethan. As of yesterday, we do know that Ethan lives in our community.

As we were driving out of our development, Griffin began jumping up and down (more than usual) in the backseat yelling, "Hi, Ethan! Hi, Ethan! Hi, Ethan! Hi, Ethan!"

The windows of the car were closed, and Ethan could not hear Griffin. However, I could see Ethan. From the looks of it, Ethan is a thug. He looked to be about six feet tall and was wearing those shorts that sag so low you could see his boxers and a tight white tank top usually seen on episodes of *Cops*. While Griffin was cheerfully shouting from the backseat, Ethan was repeatedly punching a smaller boy in the chest.

I was tempted to point out to Griffin that Ethan's idea of hanging out looks kinda painful. Nevertheless, it doesn't make a lick of a difference because Griffin will not be hanging out with Ethan. Ever.

The Ladies Man

Weather permitting, Griffin and I take walks together. "Weather permitting" in Florida means we get to walk approximately four times a century. Since we both have physical limitations, our strolls are usually slow and leisurely. Very slow and very leisurely, and we never go very far. Just a limping, sweating, overweight, bald, tattooed guy creeping along with his hand flapping, giggling goofball of a son. It's an image that might not make the cover of a sentimental Hallmark card, but it works for us.

The slow pace is fine by me because it gives us more time to talk. Since Griffin seems centered and focused at these times, a few weeks ago I used one of our walks as an opportunity to teach Griffin the art of conversation.

Since he is entering middle school in the fall, I pointed out to him that not all kids his age like to talk about the weather, elevators, and lunch menus. After his initial shock wore off, Griffin incredulously listened while I told him some kids like to talk about TV shows (other than Storm Chaser Stories), pop music, sports, and video games. Since he has no interest, whatsoever, in any of these topics, I tried to give him some conversation starters—ice breakers and opening lines, so to speak.

The next day, on the car ride to school, Griffin practiced his lines like a lounge lizard on the way to Studio 54 in 1978. He quietly muttered over and over again, "What is your favorite television show?"

"Do you like sports?"

"What music do you like?"

When Griffin arrived at school that day he ran out of the car and over to the first friend he saw and blurted,

"Whatisyourfavoritetelevisionshowdoyoulikesportswhatmusicdoyoulike? I like to watch Wake Up with Al on the Weather Channel! Mexican Pizza!"

So much for my little ladies' man living his father's dream of being a modern-day Casanova. Some dreams die hard. Not this one.

Grab a Shovel

Big Daddy is about to impart to you everything you need to know about friendship. In my mind you have acquaintances, bearable coworkers, more-than-waving-neighbors, hobby-specific friends, and then you have truly, deeply committed friendships.

The deep friendships are those I call *shovel ready*. These are the people that, when you call them up at 3:00 A.M. and tell them you have a dead body in the trunk of your car, their first (and only response) is, "I'll grab my shovel."

I have only one shovel-ready friend in the world— my wife. My daughter, who is ten, is coming up the ranks real fast, but I would never ask her to bury a body with me. Although we would have a good time doing it if I did.

This subject got me imagining what that hypothetical phone call in the wee hours of the morning would actually look like if it became a reality. This is how I envision the reaction to the dead body in the trunk phone call would go at the Big Daddy Home.

Mrs. Big Daddy would grab her shovel and a Pepsi, and run out the door in her PJs. She, of course, would have to go back inside and search frantically for her keys.

Lil Sis would put on the perfect grave-digging outfit with matching hat and purse. She would also grab her flashlight since every contraption that emits light in our house seems to migrate to her room.

Griffin would call the authorities and go back to sleep.

Keep Your Pants On

I bet most parents of thirteen-year-olds don't have the following conversation:

"Griffin, you need to keep your pants on while your sister's friend is over."

"Me?"

"No, the other Griffin that lives here and likes to take off his pants. Yes, you."

"But why?"

"Because your sister's friend is coming over."

"I like to take my pants off."

"I know you like to take your pants off, but just keep them on while company is here."

"Me?"

"Arrrgh!"

"I love you, Daddy."

"I love you, too, Griff. Just keep your pants on."

Fortunately, he usually keeps his pants on in mixed company, but as soon as the door slams behind our guests, it's right back to a long tee shirt and his Fruit of the Loom boxers.

Why Are You Awake?

Friends of Big Daddy

It's All Fun and Games Until Someone Learns a Lesson

By Kayleen Mendenhall

"But Moooom! I was going to pick the blue Cootie!" My four-year-old daughter crossed her arms angrily and sat glaring at me.

"You know how this game works," I answered back. "You have to roll a one in order to pick a body."

"But I *did* roll a one," she snapped back irritably.

It was true. She had. Kind of.

A moment earlier, she had flung the dice across the living room floor. And when she thought I wasn't looking, she flipped it over so that only one dot was showing. She didn't think I saw it. But I did.

"Hey, that's cheating!" I laughed. "We have to play fair, or we can't play at all."

Scowling, she handed the dice back to me. And the very next turn, I happened to roll a one.

I picked the blue Cootie. I knew it was her favorite. And, normally, I would have left it for her in lieu of another color. She knew it, and I knew it. But that night, I purposefully picked the blue one.

I was trying to send her a message: cheating doesn't pay off.

I'd like to think I was clever for trying to reinforce life lessons through our game playing. But in reality, playing games with my children has provided me with some of *my* most interesting reflections as a parent. And those reflections sometimes bear striking parallels to the games we play together, or those that I remember from my youth.

These are some of the things I've come to accept as true:

My children will always beat me at the game of Memory. Especially when it comes to remembering things I promised but had long since forgotten. Oddly, when it comes to picking up their toys or doing chores, they can develop amnesia quicker than I can blink.

I'm no longer afraid to ask for help. Everyone needs a get out of jail free card every once in a while.

There are days when I feel like my life is a constant game of Guess Who? Guess who tracked mud onto the carpet? Guess who pooped their pants? Guess who left the half-eaten cookie on the couch? Ironically, when it comes to answering these questions, no one has a Clue.

Regardless of how hungry their hippos are, my children sometimes stubbornly refuse to eat what you put in front of them. I just keep putting the marbles out there. I figure eventually, they'll realize that the game is a whole lot more fun with a full belly.

Picking my children's boogers is a lot like playing Operation.

I've learned to be wary of announcing "Uno!" before the game is won. My children have an uncanny ability to pull a reverse or Draw Four card out of their pocket at the last minute.

Mistakes are an inevitable part of parenting. To err is human. But to say "Sorry!" to my kids is both divine and essential.

Some days, I find myself sliding easily down the chute. Other days, I feel like I'm climbing that ladder. Again. And Again. I figure at least my butt's getting a good workout with all of that climbing.

I often find myself pulled in myriad directions like a game of Twister gone awry. It's those times that I need to focus on putting my right hand on red and keep my finger on what's really important. The rest of my body will follow.

Trying to contain a barrel full of monkeys can be pointless. Sometimes, all I can do is sit back, have a beer, and try my best to keep the monkeys from tangling up.

Sometimes I need to remember to throw away the instructions and create my own rules.

By the way, those that may have thought I was a mean parent for snagging the coveted blue Cootie may be pleased to know that the game took an interesting twist after that. A few rolls later, my daughter got to choose the pink Cootie. And after that, she proceeded to go on a dice rolling hot streak that made me consider getting on a plane and taking her to Vegas. The kid was on fire.

As my daughter ran around the room, brandishing her completed pink Cootie in glee, I realized that she was reinforcing a lesson I need to remember more often.

It's a game. Remember to enjoy it.

Kayleen Mendenhall is an IT geek, Web designer, artist and mother by day. She writes about her adventures in parenting at her blog, chipandbobo.com. By night, she is a beer drinker, blogger, and Hungry Hippo expert. Somewhere in between, she does laundry—lots of it.

Gladys Kravitz

Nosy Neighbor

As I sit down to write this post, Griffin can't keep away. He needs, at all costs, to see what's on my computer screen. He strains, cranes, and contorts to get a better view. He peers in from strange angles around the house. No matter how many times I tell him it is none of his business, he keeps coming back. Questioning. Inquiring. Squinting as he approaches me so I might think he really isn't looking. All with this huge smile plastered on his freckled face.

For the first few years of his life Griffin wanted little to do with our world and spent precious few moments in it. Now he has turned into Gladys Kravitz, the nosy neighbor from the 1960s sitcom *Bewitched*. He is like Big Daddy's personal paparazzi. Always on the beat. Involved in every conversation.

Like I have done several times already since paragraph one of this post, I must tell him "None of your business" a thousand times a day. I am thinking of setting up the yellow tape police use to cordon off a crime scene around my desk and phone. Uh oh, here he comes again. Got to go.

Pencil Me In

I have blogged often of Griffin's unhealthy interest in my schedule. He needs to know what I am doing at all times. It's flattering and creepy…mainly creepy.

The other day I went to pick him up at school and, on the way to my car, got the mail so I could have something to do while I waited for him to come out. When I saw him prancing out of the school (yes, he prances) I shoved the mail in the crease between the passenger seat and the center console.

Upon entering the vehicle, his typical questioning me about my day began. I guess he needs to make sure I stuck with the itinerary I provided him earlier. When I finished confirming that I pretty much stuck to the plan, he glanced at the mail shoved in the crease. Interrogation follows:

Griffin: "What is this, Daddy?"

Me: "It's the mail buddy. I was going through it while I waited for you to come out of school."

Griffin: "But, but, but, but why you get the mail? Mail was not in your plans. What time you get the mail?"

Me: "I don't know, Griff. I just got it. Not every little thing I do is in my plans. I also farted earlier. Do I need to pass that by you too?"

-Pause-

Griffin: "Daddy?"

Me: "What buddy?"

Griffin: "What time you fart?"

The Plan

I've mentioned before how Griffin shows much more interest in me than in just about anyone else. He is constantly monitoring my movements (which aren't very fast or far), phone calls (few and far between), and interactions with other people (virtually nonexistent). Don't get me wrong—

he is still a momma's boy through and through. But he has this fascination with me that is just odd. Especially since I'm not that interesting.

The other night he took a break from watching vintage FBI warning screens on YouTube to join Mrs. Big Daddy and me in the living room. Once he finished asking us about our favorite elevator manufacturers we had the following chat:

Griffin: "Daddy, what's your plan for tomorrow?"

Me: "I'm gonna sleep in, and then I have a doctor's appointment at eleven. After that I'll probably come home and nap until you guys get home from school. What's your plan."

Griffin: "School."

Then Mrs. Big Daddy tries to join the conversation hoping Griffin will acknowledge her presence in the room.

Mrs. BD: "Do you want to know what I'm doing tomorrow?"

Griffin: "No."

He then stumbles back into his room to do who-knows-what on the computer. The funny part about this exchange is that Mrs. Big Daddy's schedule is much more packed with interesting events than mine. Yet he only seems curious about Big Daddy's plans.

In any event, I'm tempted to start making stuff up just so he doesn't catch on to the fact that I've morphed into a total loser in middle age. So, if you happen to hear a cute red-headed autistic kid talking about how his dad is having lunch at the Four Seasons with Jessica Alba and Megan Fox tomorrow, there is no need to alert the tabloids (or Mrs. Big Daddy for that matter).

The Wheels on the Car

The other morning I had an appointment to take Mrs. Big Daddy's vehicle in for service at the dealership. The plan was to take it in after dropping Griffin off at school and then wait for it to be done. Even though it does not affect him in any way, Griffin insists on being informed well in advance of such appointments. It does not matter that he will be in school. He needs to know what I am doing at all times. My schedule is of critical importance to him.

For whatever reason, I forgot to notify the boy of my appointment and, since telling him the morning of the event would risk an extensive interrogation or, worse, a catastrophic meltdown, I decided to sneak this one by him. Unfortunately, Griffin saw me carry a magazine and my notebook (for post ideas) out to the car that morning. The interrogation was off and running.

Griffin: What are you doing after you bring me to school?"

Me: "Nothing much. Probably going back home."

Griffin: "Why you say probably? Why you have your notebook?"

Me: "I don't know. I might want to write down funny stuff you say."

Griffin: "While you are driving me to school? You are going to write funny stuff while you are driving?"

Me: "Um, I don't know. I just brought it. I'm not sure why."

Griffin: "Are you going to read your magazine while you are driving me to school?"

This line of questioning continued for about three or four more traffic lights until guilt (about lying to him), exhaustion, and frustration took over.

Me: "Aaaarrrghh. Okay, Griff. I am actually going to take Mommy's car in for service after I drop you off at school. That's why I brought the notebook and magazine. So I would have something to do while I waited."

The moment the words left my mouth, I regretted it. I should've kept lying to the kid. There were only a few more blocks to go, and he would have been at school, none the wiser of my trip to the dealership. But no, I had to blurt it out. At this point, his interrogation took on a new fervor and direction.

Griffin: "Is her car broken? What does *services* mean?"

Me: "Her car is fine. It just needs the oil changed and air in the tires. Stuff like that."

Griffin: "But, but, but, but there *is* air in the tires."

Me: "I know. They just check the air and other stuff."

Griffin: "Are you getting new air in the tires? Why do the tires need new air? What is wrong with the old air in the tires?"

Me: "Um, it's not really new air. They just make sure the tires have enough air in them. And they check the oil and stuff like that."

Griffin: "I like the air in the tires. I do not want new air. Why you put your hand on your forehead Daddy? Why are you giggling? Do you need to calm down?"

For the next several minutes, between his rapid-fire questions about tires and air, I tried my best to explain what getting a vehicle serviced meant. Finally, as he got out of the car at school, he cheerfully exclaimed, "Have fun with the tires, Daddy!"

Safe at First

I sometimes feel a bit like Derek Jeter. No, it's not the multimillion dollar contract, boyish good looks, or hall of fame baseball talent. It's because I am constantly hearing a play-by-play of almost every moment of my day. Griffin likes to narrate. It's like the annoying voiceover in the movie previews explaining to the audience what's going on, even when not much is happening.

For example, I was printing out some sort of insurance form the other day and I heard, in the background: "Daddy is printing. He is using his printer."

This brilliant commentary was not made to anyone in particular and didn't appear to serve any purpose. He just seems to like to talk about what I am doing. It's as though I am living every day of my life with Bob Costas in the Olympic Village.

After I finished printing, and answered a barrage of questions about the printing, I went to my room to get dressed. As I closed the door behind me, I heard: "Daddy is putting his dress on."

I want to clarify that, I do not wear dresses, although I would look fabulous if I did. Rather, any time anyone adorns any article of clothing, Griffin refers to it as "putting a dress on." Occasionally, in the case of Mrs. Big Daddy, he is right. More often than not, with me, he is wrong. Big Daddy prefers skirts with cute little blouses.

Then, as I was heading out the door (wearing an Ironman T-shirt and basketball shorts), I heard him announce,

"Daddy forgot his keys. Ooooh. He is coming back upstairs for his keys. Did you forget your keys, Daddy?"

Like my cell phone and computer usage, no one in the house seems to get the same attention from Griffin as I do. His curiosity about Big Daddy is growing daily. I guess I should be flattered he finds me interesting enough to do a play-by-play of my every move. At least I have one thing in common with Mr. Jeter. Two, if you count the boyish good looks.

Are You Using That

Big Daddy does not run. Ever. As far as self-propelled locomotion goes, I have two speeds—meander and waddle. To put this into 1970s TV terms, when I meander, I look like Huggy Bear approaching Starsky's Grand Torino with a hot tip. When I waddle, I'm all like Boss Hog chasing those crazy Duke boys while trying not to mess up my white three-piece suit.

The other day, after eating fast food, I felt a sudden urge to spend some time in the bathroom. The feeling came on quite quickly and, as I was waddling toward the powder room, my personal paparazzi stopped me for a comment on the recent bowel-related development. The interview, in its entirety, is as follows:

Griffin: "Why you running around, Daddy?"

Me: "I have to go to the bathroom."

Griffin: "But, but, but, but the bathroom is that way."

Me: "I know, I just wanted to get my magazine first."

-Pause-

Griffin: "Are you going to use your magazine in the bathroom?"

My imagination ran wild with that last question. Since I am not sure how Griffin thought I was planning on using the magazine, even though I was in a bit of a rush to reach my porcelain destination, I took the time to answer his query in a way that left no doubt.

Me: "Um, yes, Griff, I'm going to read my *Forbes* magazine in the bathroom."

Now, thanks to Griffin's unique way of phrasing his questions and my overwhelming need to share everything on this blog, you all know that I read in the bathroom. I will, however, let you know that I stop using magazines in any other way when I was about seventeen.

Touché

Griffin's obsession with my cell phone is well documented and is driving me crazy. Every time it rings he needs to know who is calling. He has a certain radar so that no matter where in the house he is, he comes running whenever I think of picking up the device. Anyone who calls me is sure to hear me yell, a few dozen times, "None of your business!"

This morning Griffin runs into the bathroom to tell me that his sister was on the phone. Feigning interest, I inquired as to who he thought had called her. I really didn't care, but I like to engage Griffin in conversations that don't involve the weather, Wilford Brimley, elevators, and/or my cell phone whenever the opportunity arises. Our conversation went something like this:

Griffin: "Daddy, Lil Sis is on the phone."

Me: "Oh. Who is she talking to?"

Griffin: "None of your business."

Me: "Touché, Griff. Touché."

Rest Area

Friends of Big Daddy

Actually, It's Cool. Go Ahead and Destroy My House.
By Jill Herschman

I have two beautiful boys: Child 1 is eight and has autism. Child 2 is five and OMGDOESN'T. When Child 1 was in kindergarten, I was chatting with another parent who was studying SPED and who told me that a mentor of hers had done some research where he followed kids with autism from diagnosis to adulthood. In that study he found that a number of those kids, when they were older, tested "off the spectrum," and that all of those kids shared the same three things in common:

1. They all had at least one parent who was very involved in their "treatment."

2. Both of their parents had stayed together.

3. They had a younger sibling who was NT.

Now, my memory here is bad, and I'm sorry but I have no more information for you than what I've said because I'm sure some of you now have questions. This is obviously not a scientific study, and it was only told to me to emphasize point number three. Child 2 was about two at the time, but we already knew that he was definitely not on the spectrum, so she was trying to make some predictions about the long-term prognosis for Child 1.

Children 1 & 2 don't really play together; Child 1 usually prefers to do his own thing, and even though Child 2 tries to engage him, it's usually a futile effort, and he tends to give up easily. So when they do play together, I'm always THRILLED, even if it means having to stay out of it while they destroy things.

So, the other night hubs and I were playing Rock Band (LOVE ROCK BAND), and the boys were "up to no good," as it were. They had found a bucket of various sized balls and were throwing them all over the TV room. Things were crashing, it was loud, and they were both laughing hysterically. At one point, man I wish I had been able to get my camera out in time, they were both crawling on the ground trying to find a ball that had gotten stuck behind a table. They were, yes, destroying the room; things were falling and possibly breaking, but they were playing together and laughing, and I was fine with that. It didn't last long—these things never do, but for about five to ten minutes there they were just brothers doing what brothers do. I'm okay with cleaning up after that.

Jill Herschman blogs at yeahgoodtimes.blogspot.com because lots of random stuff goes through her head throughout the normal course of a day, and she needs a place to put it. Mostly she just rambles incoherently about nothing. She also curses a lot.

Sensory Overload in Stim City

Stim City

Griffin stims for a good portion of every day. I am always amazed that he doesn't lose weight from all the perpetual motion. As an infant, he started with hand twisting. It was as though he was using imaginary screwdrivers with both hands simultaneously, trying to screw forty-foot-long screws into kryptonite. This morphed into arm and hand flapping like a bird. Some days, during this stage, we thought he would fly away. Through the years, he has had so many facial tics and stims we can't even count. Now his stim of choice is the maniacal laugh I've posted about before, accompanied by some serious belly slapping. He also likes to rub the outside of his hand raw on his shirt. Fun stuff.

We have learned that trying to suppress his stims is futile. When one appears to subside, another always seems to emerge. Usually the new one leaves us pining for the old one. When we hear him howling at 120 decibels at three in the morning, oh how we miss the double-fisted-screw-driver-twisters from the late '90s.

When in public we try to have him keep the stims in check as much as possible. Because we know this is such a struggle for him, we try to make home a complete sanctuary for Griffin. He knows he can completely let loose at home. Cackling, hand flapping, jumping, yelling, and barfing are never out of the question. The noises wafting from our house must make our neighbors wonder what kind of evil experiments we are conducting on our kids.

I can't wait to see what emerges once the maniacal laugh and belly slapping subsides. No. Really. I can't wait.

Stop the Hug

The first time Griffin hugged me I mean really hugged me—was the day his sister was born. He was almost three, and it was the first day and night he had been away from Mrs. Big Daddy. I guess he figured I was a suitable substitute for his mommy who had been receiving hugs from him for some time. As a baby he was always rigid and never seemed to relax his body for a true, meaningful embrace. He is still real sensitive to touch. However, he now gives some of the best hugs around.

I pretty much get hugs on demand. Most of the time he will back in or come to me sideways with his head lowered to give me a half-assed hug. But if I tell him I want a "big squeezy hug," he turns to me, throws his arms around my neck, and comes in for a full-body embrace. He usually only lets the hug last for a few seconds. I hold on until he pulls away. I waited a long time to get these hugs so I make them last.

When he has had enough he usually says, "Stop the hug!"

It's as though he is on a merry-go-around and is asking the ride operator to shut it down so he could get off and grab some cotton candy. Nowadays, like an underpaid carnival worker bent on revenge, I usually don't let go until I hear him squeal, "Stop the hug!"

It's Good to Be Big Daddy

Much like Mel Brooks smugly proclaimed about being the king in *History of the World Part I*, it's good to be Big Daddy. While I alone endure the constant scrutiny of my phone calls, bathroom habits, and computer usage, Griffin treats me better than he does Mrs. Big Daddy in certain other respects. Napping comes to mind.

My love of napping is well known in Casa de Big Daddy. I try to take at least one every day. If you told our neighbors that, they'd think you're nuts since the noises emanating from Griffin can be heard miles away. You too might wonder how I can nap in such a mad house.

I can and do nap because Griffin is able, somehow, to turn off the maniacal laughing and loud belly slapping whenever he knows I am heading for my mid-afternoon slumber. I have no idea how he does it, but he does. When he senses I am on my way into the arms of Morpheus, this conversation usually occurs:

Griffin: "Are going to take a nap, Daddy?"

Me: "Yup."

Griffin: "Can I be quiet?"

Me: "I hope so."

Griffin: "Why you say *hope* Daddy?"

Me: "I don't know, Griff."

Griffin: "Why you say *I don't know*, Daddy."

Me: "Not sure how to answer that, Griff. I'm just sleepy."

Griffin: "I will try to be quiet."

And he usually is. Not only does he monitor his own noise levels, he makes sure everyone else does as well. As soon as I close my door, I can hear him running around the house like a little Paul Revere telling Mrs. Big Daddy and Lil Sis that they cannot disturb Daddy because he is taking a nap.

If Mrs. Big Daddy dares to enter the bedroom to put away some laundry or use the bathroom, Griffin is on her like a Secret Service agent on John Hinckley. I smile sleepily as I hear:

Griffin: "No, no, no, no do not disturb Daddy!"

Mrs. BD: "Griff, this is my room, too, and I have put away the laundry."

Griffin: (Standing in front of the door) "No, no, no, no do not disturb Daddy!"

Mrs. BD: (huffing) "Fine!"

On the rare occasion that Mrs. Big Daddy tries to take a nap, she gets no such respect. The Count is in the house, and he doesn't even lighten up on his usual barrage of questions. He will actually walk by me sitting in the kitchen to go ask his napping mom for a snack. Now that's respect.

Sometimes it's good to be Big Daddy.

All Thumbs

Several years ago we became concerned about the frequency of Griffin's headaches and a new stim he developed that looked to his teachers at school like a seizure. We checked him into a hospital for neurological tests that ultimately allayed our concerns. Somewhat.

However, while at the hospital, of all the indignities, inconveniences, and outright painful experiences he had to endure, it was the pulse monitor gently clipped on his thumb that most bothered Griffin. Every time they clipped it on, he would complain bitterly and remove it. CT scans,

MRIs, and IVs didn't upset him in the least, but the thumb clip was too much.

Now, whenever Griffin learns that someone has been to the hospital, his main concern is the condition of their digitus primus. After I returned home from a weeklong stay in the ICU with an episode of pancreatitis, Griffin welcomed me with a big old hug and a concerned, "Daddy, is your thumb feeling better?" Actually, my thumb was fine, but I didn't have the heart to tell him that my thumb was virtually the *only* thing that was feeling remotely better. But the hug from Griffin sure helped.

During one of my more recent stays in the hospital, Mrs. Big Daddy brought the kids to visit me. Griffin's behavior was a bit odd, even for him. Specifically, he refused to look at me. He entered the room walking backwards and kept his back to me the whole visit.

He carried on normal (for him) conversations with me about the weather and elevator videos, but he never faced me. When I made him give me a kiss good-bye, he came in with his face all squished up squinting out of one eye just so he wouldn't knock over the IV stand. He looked like a pirate who hadn't pooped in a week.

My theory is that he didn't want to look at me because, in his mind, as long as he never saw me lying in the hospital bed, I wasn't really sick. That, or he is just autistic, and we may never know why he does certain things. Griffin was, however, very interested in the IV drip. He asked, with his body still turned away from me:

Griffin: "Why you have that bag of water there?"

Me: "It's not water, Griff. It's saline. It's my food while I am in here."

After a brief pause he queried:

Griffin: "Does it taste like a cheeseburger?"

Me: "I wish. Now turn around and give me a big squeezy hug."

Say Fake

Friends of Big Daddy

Mad Hatter

By Caryn Black Haluska

Somehow, in a previous life, I must have been an amazingly awesome person. This is the only reason I can think of for explaining how lucky I am to have Logan. My two year old holds my heart in his hand and has the rest of me wrapped around his tiny little finger.

It's true that he is on the autism spectrum, and has sensory processing disorder. Because of these things and other issues, he has a bit of a rough time. But it's also true that he is one of the funniest people I know. He can make me laugh with just a look. I feel it is only fair that I share the funny little things he does with others to make the world a brighter, happier place.

Logan becomes extremely attached to odd things. He loves *nekkiss* (anything that has a cord so it can be worn around the neck). He is obsessed with puppies. But last night he formed a new attachment never before seen at the Monster House. He found the top to our hot air popcorn popper in the back of a kitchen cupboard. I have no idea how he figured this next part out, but he discovered that it fit on his head perfectly. He could shake his head from side to side as hard as he could, and it would not fly off. So, he did. He shook his head until he was dizzy, giggling all the while. Then he would take a minute for the world to stop spinning and do it all over again.

If it had stopped there, it would have still been funny. But there's more! The popper top made him look like the Lego man, ready to have another giant Lego snapped on the top of his head. Every time I looked at him, I got the giggles. Pictures were taken, and we bribed him shamelessly to perform as the Lego man. And then, it was time for bed.

We tried to take the Lego man popper top off him. There was screaming. There was kicking. There were shrieks of "GO 'WAY!" and "NO TOUCH!" He took his bath with it on. He dried off, got into pajamas, and had his snack while wearing it. After two hours of hysterics, we let him fall asleep with it on. I found myself sneaking into the nursery to peek at him, hoping it would fall off his head during the night. No such luck. The thing was snug, and he amazingly slept all night for the first time in weeks.

This morning, when I took him out of the crib, he handed me the "hat" and said, "Ah Done." And that was that. Except for a slightly movie theater butter scented head...you would never know that a hot air popcorn popper top had been his best friend.

Caryn Black Haluska is a mother of seven cuddly monsters. When her youngest was diagnosed with sensory processing disorder and pervasive developmental disorder, she channeled her copywriting experience into blogging at www.livingwithlogan.com, where she shares glimpses into the amusing antics at the "Monster House," as well as information about interventions, gf/cf cooking, and the importance of family. Caryn shares her ups and downs of living with special needs in her unique voice that will inspire you to look at your own monster house through new eyes.

Hello?

Wrong Number

I have written often about Griffin's obsession with my cell phone. It truly is one of life's great mysteries why he is so interested in my cell, which rings approximately three times a week while he ignores Mrs. Big Daddy's Blackberry which bings, beeps, blips, buzzes, bongs, rings, zings, and clangs every two minutes.

When I've tired of telling him its none of his business who called, I resort to lying to him. I tell him it's just a wrong number. Sometimes this is actually true. The first few times I used this ploy he fell for it like I fell for Mrs. Big Daddy's lasagna the first time I tasted it. Hook line and sinker. Nowadays he is not buying into the fib so readily. After a brief conversation with a person I barely know on a topic that is so trivial I cannot even remember it now, I was involuntarily made a part of the following impromptu press conference:

Griffin: "Who was that Daddy?"

Me: "No one. It was just a wrong number, Griff."

Griffin: "But, but, but I heard you talking."

Me: "Don't worry. It was just a wrong number."

Griffin: "But I heard you say 'Hi, Hilary. How are you?' Was Hilary a wrong number? Who is Hilary, Daddy?"

Me: "I, um, no Hilary is not a wrong number. She called about a deposit I made at the bank …ugh! It's none of your business, Griffin."

Griffin: "Was is it an accident? Was Hilary a wrong number? What's a deposbit?"

Me: "Argh."

I wish, like a politician, I could have some assistant jump in and tell the pesky reporter that the press conference is over and be done with it. Worst of all, for the next week, every time I even glanced at my cell phone, Griffin would come running from where ever he was in the house, screaming, "Is that Hilary?"

We Caved

Griffin has been pestering us for a cell phone for months now. Even though he is thirteen we didn't think he needed (or could handle) one. This is especially true since his stated reason for wanting a phone was to call "his girls." As I have mentioned in posts past, there is an ever growing group of girls at school who treat Griffin like a rock star and whom, like a ghetto pimp, he refers to as "his girls."

Our fear was that one of these poor young ladies would actually give him her number and then Big Daddy would be forced to learn all about telephone and text stalking laws. Have I mentioned that Griffin doesn't really get social cues or hints?

Lil Sis is already on her second cell phone since she got her first one when she was nine. In an uncharacteristic use of logic, Griffin pointed out that it wasn't fair that his little sister had a phone and he, the teenager, did not. When we pointed out that he did not know how to use the phone, he continued with the baffling logic by implying his sister could teach him. The deal was sealed when Griffin agreed to a *contacts lock* whereby he could only call and text family members and contacts that we approve and that the approved list most definitely would not include any of his girls or Wilford Brimley.

So, for his birthday, we got him a phone, and Mrs. Big Daddy plugged in the ten or so contacts he is allowed to reach out and touch. With a few quick lessons from Lil Sis, he was able to figure out how to slide out the keyboard and text away. Not surprisingly, I'm his favorite target. Over the past several days I have received the following missives:

"There is a elevator near Lumix14 is the Witha center."

"Dear daddy check the money and the bank free credit score."

"How was your money daddy and pay taxes."

"Have you heard from thegrudge58."

You may think, from the content of his texts, that we wasted our money getting him a phone, but the look on his face when he unwrapped it was well worth it. Besides, now I don't have to even get up from the couch to tell him to quiet down when he is maniacally laughing in his room. I just text him.

Inches

When we got Griffin his cell phone we clearly told him that the only people he would be able to contact were family members. We configured the phone such that there would be no way he could contact anyone who might call the police or seek a restraining order against him. This has worked fairly well but now Griffin is protesting a bit.

He wants to call and text his friends. By friends, he means the group of girls at school who say hello to him and treat him nicely. This is a sweet group of girls to whom we are eternally grateful for their treatment of Griffin. However, we would not want to subject them to a constant barrage of texts about elevator videos and requests for play dates.

Griffin disagrees. While not persuasive, his arguments are unique.

Griffin: "I want to call my girls."

Me: "You know the rules."

Griffin: "But, but, but, but, I want to call my girls."

Me: "You are not a big enough boy yet to have that privilege."

Griffin: "But, but, but, but, I am big."

Me: "Not big enough. You need to show us you are a big enough boy to be able to text or call your friends."

Griffin: "But, but, but, but, Lil Sis calls her friends. I am bigger than her."

Me: "Ugh. I know you are bigger than her size wise, but she is more mature with the phone. Once you mature, you can call your friends."

Griffin" "How many more inches until I am mature?"

Trying the Side Door

We've been getting a lot of calls from telemarketers recently. This is not a good thing since I live in a house with an autistic boy who freaks out whenever the phone rings and needs to know every detail about every phone call involving his father in any way, shape, or form. So I decided to put our number on the government's Do Not Call List.

I've done this before with other phone numbers, but couldn't remember the precise Web address to sign up our new number. Instead spending about ten seconds doing a Google search, I e-mailed a buddy of mine (we'll call him Bob) who knows all about such things. About an hour later, while driving in the car with Griffin, Bob got back to me. I checked the e-mail on my Blackberry, and the interrogation by Griffin began. Griffin tried every which way to get me to tell him what the e-mail from Bob was about.

Griffin: "Who e-mailed you, Daddy?"

Me: "None of your business."

Griffin: "It was Bob. I saw it was from Bob. What did Bob e-mail you about?"

Me: "None of your business."

Griffin: "Did Bob e-mail you about something?"

Me: "None of your business."

Griffin: "When Bob e-mailed you, was it about something?"

Me: "None of your business."

After about ten minutes of him rephrasing the same question and then expecting me to fall for his ruse and give him the information he so desperately wanted, I had had enough. I told him if he asked me another question about the e-mail from Bob, he would lose computer privileges for the day.

After a few moments of silence he nonchalantly asked,

Griffin: "So. Daddy?"

Me: "This better not be a question about the e-mail from Bob."

Griffin: "No, no, no, no. It is not about the e-mail from Bob!"

Me: "Okay. What?"

Griffin: "Earlier today, were you in your office when you sent a e-mail to Bob?"

Me: "Ugghhh!"

Griffin: "Was that e-mail you sent to Bob about something?"

Me: "Arrgghh!"

Aaaachoo Baby

Friends of Big Daddy

Acceptance
By Stuart Duncan

I used to think that accepting the idea that my son had autism was a moment of enlightenment. That moment where you've had your child diagnosed, you've put aside the denial, you've put aside the confusion, and you've accepted it for what it is.

What I've come to realize, however, is that acceptance, when dealing with autism, comes at various stages and that the moment of enlightenment I had was actually just stage two of what would be a long journey.

Here is how I break it down, from personal experience.

Stage one of acceptance actually hits you when you first recognize that there are delays. This is when you ask your doctor about getting an assessment. Perhaps it's when a day-care worker or friend or family member mentions the big A word for the first time that you make a realization. It's this realization that leads to having to accept it as a reality. Along with stage one comes a lot of denial and confusion, but you're still well on your way to having to accept your child for who they are.

Stage two is when you have the pile of papers in your hand, complete with the official diagnosis. For a while, the amount of time varies between us all, you feel lost, alone, confused...unsure what to do next, but at some point, you accept the diagnosis for what it is, and you vow to do whatever you have to do to make sure that your child won't just be another statistic...that you'll find some way to not only make it right but to love your child even if you can't.

Stage three of acceptance, the final stage, is when you realize that your fight to fix the autism has, while still very important, faded into the shadow of accepting your child for who he or she is...and what he or she has. You learn that you should love your child with autism, rather than love your child despite autism. This is a very big turning point because only when you can do this can you stop seeing your child as broken or flawed in some way.

This is a very basic and minuscule glimpse of the whole myriad of emotions and life changing experiences that you will encounter between that first day that you realize your child is missing milestone up until...well, today. But these are very important steps to take in turning something very tragic into something that simply is...your child is your child—perfect and flawed and unique and beautiful.

Stuart Duncan is a work-from-home father with two boys, one with autism and one without. Learning all he can as he pushes for autism understanding and acceptance.

Chicken Sandwich

Mexican Pizza

Occasionally, Griffin, out of nowhere, will just blurt out selections from a school lunch menu he may have been studying weeks earlier. It is not unusual for us to be driving, having a conversation that does not involve him, and hear Griffin yell, "Mexican pizza!" or "Chicken sandwich!" from the backseat.

It's not like he wanted Mexican pizza or a chicken sandwich for lunch nor was it remotely related to what we were talking about—he just felt the need to say it. Like a living, breathing pop-up ad, he does this frequently with all sorts of nouns, verbs, and adjectives. I bet Griffin's spontaneity, brevity, and randomness would make him hugely successful on Twitter.

Mrs. Big Daddy and I often wonder what's going on inside Griffin's head. She sometimes describes her theory using the analogy of an old style office Rolodex. The cards inside his mind are furiously spinning around and around. Occasionally the Rolodex stops for an instant and Griffin will blurt out whatever thought is on the selected card. Then the Rolodex starts to spin again.

I think of the bouncing balls the state lottery uses to pick the Lotto numbers on Saturday nights. All the Ping-pong balls bounce around in the air chamber. One finally pops out and that's Griffin's thought for the moment.

Either way, it's pretty hectic in there.

Tonight, on the way to dinner, Griffin got me to join in on this madness. Our conversation went like this.

Griffin: "Daddy, I ask you a question?"

Me: "Sure, Griff."

Griffin: "Say *fake*."

Me: "Fake."

Griffin: "Why you say 'fake,' Daddy?"

Me: "Argh."

Griffin: "Why you say 'argh,' Daddy?"

I think this exchange sums up our life with Griffin pretty well.

The Truman Show

Sometimes, when alone with Griffin, I find myself scanning the room for hidden cameras thinking this must be a set up like Jim Carey in *The Truman Show*. I imagine there are millions of people watching us and having a great laugh at whatever bizarre comment just came out of his mouth. I wouldn't be surprised to see Alan Funt coming through the door yelling, "Smile, you're on *Candid Camera*."

I So Sweaty

Walking around an indoor flea market the other day, it struck me how perfectly Griffin would fit into one of those retirement communities in Arizona, where the old people sit around and complain all day. As we slowly walked the aisles full of junk, I heard Griffin say to no one in particular, over a period of maybe ten or fifteen seconds:

"I so sweaty."

"My knees hurt."

"It smells funny in here."

This monologue, along with the way he shuffles along at a snail's pace in his flip-flops, makes me think he would be right at home in a mah-jongg tournament on Miami Beach.

I Need Ice

Griffin gets headaches after spending too much time in the "real world" trying to be "normal" for the benefit of a sometimes callous and noncaring public. When he gets such a headache, the only remedy that helps is a freezer bag full of ice on top of his head.

Griffin gallops around relatively gracefully while balancing the homemade ice pack on his cranium. The ice does not inhibit his regular activities in the least. He even plays on the computer and straps his headphones on over the bag. This is an impressive feat of coordination for a kid who can't put on his own socks, runs like Herman Munster, and regularly dances like Elaine Benes from Seinfeld.

Recently, after one particularly rough day in public, Griffin was in desperate need of some ice. I was standing next to the refrigerator when he stumbled by me in search of his mommy, who was just getting out of the shower.

Upon reaching the master bathroom and seeing his mom, Griffin blurted out the only two things on his mind at the that precise moment in time,

"I SEE YOU NAKED! I NEED ICE!"

Now we all knew those two phrases were not related. Griffin did not need ice because he saw his mommy naked. He needed ice because he had a headache. His mommy happened to be naked because that is how most people take a shower. However, that unfortunate confluence of circumstances has haunted Mrs. Big Daddy ever since. Whenever

Lil Sis or I see Mrs. Big Daddy in any stage of undress, even if it is just her kicking off her flip-flops, we simultaneously yell, "I NEED ICE!"

This has done wonders for Mrs. Big Daddy's self confidence and my love life. Therapy is going well, and our psychologist believes Mrs. BD may one day be able to take a shower without locking the door and turning off the lights. Griffin remains completely unaffected by the incident; although he does seem to smirk whenever Lil Sis or I tease his mother about it.

Feet Don't Fail Now

For a few weeks now Griffin has been reading for pleasure. This, obviously, is a huge development that we try to encourage as much as possible. Mostly he has been reading his sister's old books like the *Wimpy Kid* series. We are not sure how much he comprehends but, after each chapter he gives us a three- or four-word summary so we know he is actually reading each night. Like I said, we are beyond overjoyed at this new hobby.

The other evening Griffin came into the living room and announced that he wanted to skip reading that night. His reason? His feet were tired. That's right, he told us he could not read that night because his feet were too tired.

Dreams

Griffin doesn't dream. Or so he says. Most nights, before he goes to bed, he proclaims: "I will not dream tonight."

I have no idea whether it is just wishful thinking on his part or he can actually turn off his dream cycle at will. I know that, at least on some nights, he does dream because several months ago he came bounding into my bedroom way too early in the morning yelling, "Last night I dreamed

Barney was at the Weather Channel talking about severe weather alerts in the northeast! Do you believe that?!?"

I definitely believed it. Since the Barney dream, I had not heard of any other dreams until a few nights ago, as we were entering Longhorn to celebrate his Poppy's birthday, he quietly told me,

"Last night I dreamed you were on the phone with Poppy. But it was not Poppy."

I tried to get more details, to no avail. Apparently, his obsession with my phone follows him into slumber as well.

Louder

I know it's not uncommon for autistic kids to parrot or mimic what is said to them. We went through this stage with Griffin. However, nowadays, the boy has turned it around on us. Many times he will implore other family members to repeat the random stuff that spews out of his mouth on a regular basis.

Many people have witnessed the Big Daddy clan cruising down the highway gleefully saying (for no apparent or logical reason whatsoever),

"Chicken sandwich"

or

"Are you in good hands?"

or

"Call now."

It makes him happy, so we oblige.

Taking him to school the other day, the game took an unexpected turn.

Griffin: "Daddy, say Now for the weekend weather."

Me: (In my weather person voice) "Now for the weekend weather."

Griffin: "Louder, Daddy, louder!"

Me: "NOW FOR THE WEEKEND WEATHER!"

Griffin: "Ooo. Why you yelling, Daddy? Stop talking so loud."

Me: "Ugghh."

Wilford, Me, and the Burger King

They say there are no coincidences in life so I guess I shouldn't be shocked that Griffin has formed a bond with Wilford Brimley, of diabetes supplies fame. Big Daddy has had diabetes for about fifteen years now. In reality, I don't have diabetes so much as diabetes has me. I was first diagnosed when I was in my early thirties. Recently, more often than not, diabetes has kicked my ass.

Because of my condition, I see my endocrinologist fairly regularly. The day before Thanksgiving was no different. The girls—Lil Sis, Mrs. Big Daddy, and Big Nana—had plans for a girls-only outing so I had to take Griffin with me to my appointment.

My endocrinologist appointments are no big deal. He is usually on time and the entire five-minute appointment can be summed as follows;

1. Weighs me.
2. Frowns.
3. Takes blood pressure.
4. Frowns.
5. Tells me I am fat.
6. Writes my prescriptions.

So bringing Griffin shouldn't have been a hassle. Just to make sure, I promised him Burger King for lunch after the appointment conditioned upon the following:

1. No loud laughing.

2. He does not mention to the endocrinologist that we would be going to Burger King.

As we entered the waiting room, Griffin was busy confirming which Burger King we would be visiting and what his order was going to be. When I reminded him of the deal, he reminded me that he did not, technically, tell it to the doctor. Hmm. At this point, I thought I had a chance of sliding through the appointment without the doctor hearing of my lunch plans.

No such luck. Griff lasted all of about thirty seconds until the cork blew out and a hot steaming river of Burger King conversation starting flowing down the side of the mountain. By the end of the appointment, my endocrinologist knew which Burger King we were going to, what Griffin was having, and the details of our plan to keep this information from the him.

The two Whoppers I later scarfed down did nothing to console me.

The Donald Duck Incident

The scene is familiar enough. Grainy black and white footage of crazed autograph-seeking fans chasing the Beatles through the streets of London, circa 1964. If you thought this type of celebrity worship has gone the way of Nehru jackets and white go-go boots, you haven't been to Walt Disney World recently.

Thousands of children visit the house that Mickey built every year. A good number of these kids convince their parents to spend $49.99 on a Disney-certified autograph pad and an official two-foot-long signature pen so that they can risk sun stroke in a quest to get "priceless" autographs from teenagers being paid minimum wage to stand around dressed up as cartoon characters. From a profit-and-loss standpoint, I must commend the Mouse on a brilliant move. Charging nearly fifty bucks for a spiral notebook and pen that cost them all of six cents to produce in China is pure genius. However, as a parent, I am revolted at the torture this scheme inflicts on us.

Waiting in DMV worthy lines in the broiling heat with cranky children, in an effort to get a worthless signature that will be thrown away before we check out of the hotel the next morning, is bad enough. Then, we are forced to endure the tantrums caused by the OSHA required breaks the characters take every four minutes. The final indignity thrust on the parents is the constant and relentless hounding to spend another $29.99 for a "professional" snapshot of our hysterical kid with his sweaty face buried in Goofy's armpit.

For many years, through numerous visits, we were able to avoid falling into this trap since our oldest child, Griffin, showed no interest. Griffin is autistic. He is not just slightly inattentive, distracted, or hyperactive. Griffin is considerably hindered and disabled by this confounding disorder. Every minute, of every day, autism is a tremendous part of our lives.

One "upside" to Griffin's disability is that we never had to endure the torture of the autograph hunt. But that came to an end when Griffin was about eleven, when his little sister talked him into participating. In no time, Chip and Dale, Minnie, Mickey, and dozens of other "celebrities" were successfully tracked, stalked, and autographs obtained without incident. Then it came time to bag the Duck.

It was early afternoon and the temperature was approaching 1,214 degrees. Perspiration was copiously gushing out of every square inch of my body. Even my ears and fingers were sweating profusely. The smell of popcorn, cotton candy, and tourist body odor filled the humid afternoon air. If the teenager (aka "cast member") in the Donald Duck suit was not already cursing the sequence of events that put him in this sauna they called a duck suit on this day, Griffin was about to add insult to injury.

Fake Donald did his best to sign the kids' books, considering his hands were covered in padded rubber and vinyl, and his only way to see the world (and breathe) was through tiny holes in his unwieldy orange plastic beak. Instead of moving along after getting Donald's autograph and enduring the obligatory photo op, Griffin just stood there looking at the page in his book for several seconds.

He then turned indignantly to Donald and exclaimed for all to hear: "I cannot read this!!"

The well-oiled Disney Machine temporarily came to a screeching halt as the other parents glared at us for holding up the line. I could almost swear the whistling theme from "The Good, the Bad, and the Ugly" was playing in the background as Griffin and Donald stared each other down. Face to face. Prosthetic bill to sunburned nose. I think a desert tumbleweed rolled by as a saloon door creaked open and shut in the distance.

Griffin drew first. When he shoved the autograph book back at the duck for a more legible signature, the rest of the world around us remained eerily still. I am sure this Donald had been poked, pinched, punched, and maybe even puked on by park guests in the past. However, it must have been particularly galling to have his penmanship critiqued by a profusely perspiring kid who, on the surface, appeared old enough to know the game.

The drama unfolded in slow motion. As a droplet of sweat leisurely rolled off Griffin's nose, I could feel the tension in the air building. Sensing imminent danger (or at least further embarrassment), I rushed in like a linebacker to physically remove Griffin from the signing pagoda. Donald was efficiently escorted away by his surprisingly large (and aggressive) entourage. It reminded of Ronald Reagan being shoved into the limo by the Secret Service after John Hinckley shot at him.

This encounter shows that Griffin can be quite literal and fairly rigid in his thinking. Figurative language, comprehension, and inference deficiencies hamper Griffin's communication ability and hinders his capacity to interact with others in society. It is Griffin's inability to pick up on social clues and abstract concepts that may keep him from ever leading a life that is completely independent of his parents. Statistically speaking, the odds of him achieving a high level of independence as an adult are slim.

Oddly, accepting this possibility has had a profoundly positive effect on our life. Now, instead of spending every waking minute trying to "fix" him, we focus on enjoying every moment with him. The first few years of his life we were so obsessed with curing him that we probably missed out on so much. Now that we accept Griffin unconditionally, life is infinitely better for all of us. We feel that we are incredibly fortunate that we may get to spend all of our years with someone who is so unique and sees the world in a way that no one else does. Donald Duck may disagree.

A Joke

Friends of Big Daddy

A Tale of Two Essays: Holland Reacts

By Lynn Hudoba

Most special needs parents are familiar with the essay "Welcome to Holland," which compares having a disabled child with planning a trip to Italy but landing in Holland instead. The premise is that Holland is a perfectly fine place too; not where you were planning on going, but you get used to it and even end up seeing the beauty in it.

Then there is the rebuttal essay called "Holland Schmolland," which takes exception to that comparison. Holland is much too nice of a place to be compared with the experience of raising a child with autism. The author makes up her own alternate country, in which the traits and symptoms of autism are considered to be the defining customs of this strange land.

I happened to have lived in the Netherlands for five years in the 90s, and always wondered how it was that Holland got thrown in to this great debate. Why Holland? It was just sitting there, all flat and neutral, minding its own. How does Holland feel about its role as the chief metaphor in these essays?

Well, even though it's been a while since I lived there, Holland and I have kept in touch, and I was able to get him to agree to an interview. I know, quite a "get," as we say in the biz. He was able to fit me in between deporting stoned frat boys and making fun of Belgium.

LYNN: Do you mind not smoking?

Holland: Yes.

LYNN: So how have you been, Holland? What's the weather like today?

Holland: Ha. Good one. Fifty degrees and raining like it is every day.

LYNN: Can you believe it's been almost eleven years since I left?

Holland: Yeah, we're still trying to get over it. We keep a light on over an empty cubby in the Red Light district just for you...sort of like your Tomb of the Unknown Soldier.

LYNN: Nice. Well, today I wanted to talk to you about these essays that compare having a special needs child with living in Holland. What do you think of them?

Holland: I guess it's not surprising that I disagree with the premise of "Welcome to Holland," which is that Holland is somehow not as desirable a destination as Italy. Please. You want to go Italy, go to Italy. Good luck making it out of the airport with your daughter's hymen intact.

LYNN: Easy! My daughter is six years old.

Holland: Oh, sorry. I thought that she was over the Italian age of consent. You know, twelve.

LYNN: What do you think about the Holland being used as a metaphor for raising a child with autism?

Holland: "Holland Schmolland" talks about raising a child with autism being like a more violence-ravaged country where it's customary for mothers to have their "boo-doos" squeezed. Which ironically brings us back to....ITALY. Are you with me, people? Actually, it would be even better if you guys would leave us all alone and stick with your own continent. If you're looking for someone that's odd, battle-scarred, and has a bum GI tract, look no further than south of your border.

LYNN: Is there any comparison that you think is valid between you and raising a child with autism?

Holland: Well, like I said, the weather here can be really lousy. Most days are gray, dreary, and depressing. But every so often, a day comes along that is just breathtakingly beautiful. The clouds part, the sun comes streaming through, and you appreciate it all the more for all the rainy days that you've endured. The terraces come alive, everyone pulls a chair out from inside, peels off their layers, and we all raise our faces to the sun and soak in every last second of it before the clouds come along to blot it out again.

LYNN: That's really beautiful.

Holland: Yeah, I thought you'd like that. I got plenty more cheese where that came from.

LYNN: You just couldn't leave it alone, could you?

Lynn Hudoba is the mother of an amazing little girl who happens to have autism. Her blog, "My Life as an Ungraceful, Unhinged, and Unwilling Draftee Into the Autism Army," can be found at www.autismarmymom.com. Follow this mother and daughter as they take the road less traveled, dance to a different drummer, and lots of other clichés that describe their unique, unexpected, and often hilarious journey.

Let's Have Some Preachiness

At the outset, I said that I would not be providing too much practical advice or resources. However, you may have noticed that sporadically I broke that promise and provided some tricks of the trade. Further, as I plowed through this project, I realized that there were a ton of lessons we learned that may be helpful for other parents in our position. Raising a disabled child can be a baffling and overwhelming prospect. We would be remiss not to pass along what we have gleaned through trial and error.

The following is a brief summary of the top eleven principles we have found to help us along in our journey.

The List

1. Acceptance. Our lives changed for the better when we acknowledged the situation and then decided what we're going to do about it. We feel as though acceptance is being able to embrace what is rather than constantly wishing for what is not and what can never be. Just because we accept Griffin's condition does not mean we are thrilled about it or that we wouldn't prefer it to be different. By accepting it, we take the first step toward making the best of the situation. We can then get on with the business of changing what we can and learning how to live with that which we cannot. If we never took that initial step of acceptance, we would have been stuck,

and if we never accepted our circumstances, we never would have known if any part of it could be made better.

2. Laugh. A lot. We have discovered that, by finding and recognizing the humor in our lives, we are better able to survive it. Laughter allows us to move through tragic circumstances and is integral to our peace of mind.

3. Adapt. Griffin's difficulties have caused us to cultivate an environment of ingenuity that we frequently use to find ways to make our lives better. This applies to coming up with clever little solutions to everyday problems, as well as transforming major negative aspects of our life into positive situations. For us, our challenges have revealed a certain type of genius that would have remained hidden if not for the hardships that have been thrust on us. The rewards of not only overcoming adversity but turning that adversity into prosperity are innumerable and immense.

4. Gratitude. Gratitude changes suffering into acceptance, despair into fulfillment, difficulties into gifts, sorrow into joy, and mistakes into perfection. Gratitude lets us release the past, brings serenity for today, and gives us hope for the future. Gratitude is how we get through every day.

5. Love. Each other and yourself. Without this, none of the rest would matter in the least. Sometimes the most obvious strategies get lost in the shuffle. This is one that should never get pushed to the side.

6. Embrace optimism. We choose to be optimistic because it just feels better than wallowing in sorrow, grief, and self-pity. Optimism and pessimism are contagious. I

would rather spread hopefulness and brightness to my kids any day of the week.

7. Ask for help. If we were too timid to ask for assistance early on, we could only imagine where Griffin would be today. By seeking assistance, we do not mean forming an unhealthy dependence on any one person or thing. We have surrounded ourselves with a good team of professionals, friends, and family. This has resulted in remarkable progress for Griffin. When someone or something is not working, we replace it. Our focus is making Griffin's life (and the rest of the family's life) better with the assistance of others.

8. Don't coddle. While we do make accommodations for him, we try not to let Griffin get away with anything we know he can control or handle. He does not get any special treatment from us, and that includes getting teased and being required to pull his own weight (where physically possible) when it comes to chores and the like.

9. Be nonjudgmental. It is impossible to determine or understand what purpose or place an event or occurrence has in the big picture of the universe. When we are presented with something that, at first, appears either devastating or incredibly fortuitous, it is helpful to treat it without judgment. You really never know. Instead of judging, we just accept it and go from there.

10. Trust your gut. If it smells like a quack, looks like a quack, feels like a quack, and quacks like a quack, it's probably a quack. It's easy to get caught up in the mania caused by the rumors that occasionally float around

the community of parents of disabled kids. We are not aware of any effective miracle cure now available, and we have found that traditional therapies and medicines work best for Griffin. That's not to say that some nontraditional approaches are without merit. Some of these may work well for other kids. We just think a logical risk/benefit analysis should be undertaken before subjecting Griffin to more medical and quasi-medical procedures.

11. Avoid complacency. We firmly believe that early intervention was critical in Griffin's development. We keep moving forward. Always tinkering with his therapies and medications. By never resting on our laurels, Griffin continues to progress and grow. He is thriving.

While we have absolutely no proof these principles have made Griffin any "less autistic," we know they have made our life better. There may be no medical research to support the benefits of any of the above. However, it seems to have worked for us.

Epilogue

For the Big Daddy clan, the streets of Holland are filled with mirth and delight. We are not deluded and we recognize that our life is not easy. Instead of wallowing in a puddle of self-pity, we laugh our way out of the muck. If you allow it to be, the world can seem full of sorrows and negativity. We chose to live in joy.

Photography by: Hayden E. Korr

About the Author

F. Lewis Stark, a.k.a. Big Daddy, is the best-selling author of absolutely nothing. He spends his days writing for his blog (BigDaddyAutism.com), enjoying his kids, doing crossword puzzles, yelling at the TV, and thinking about what to eat for lunch. He has several very nice tattoos that his mother pretends don't exist. Mr. Stark is able to survive each day with the help of his long-suffering and beautiful wife, Sonya. You can reach him at <u>bigdaddyautism@gmail.com</u> as long as the cable company has not terminated his Internet service for failing to pay for Griffin's On Demand purchases.

8841268R0

Made in the USA
Charleston, SC
19 July 2011